Cosmo and Me

A Seeker's Journey from Religion to Spirituality

Jim Willis

Uncle Bear Publishing
68089 Risueno Rd.
Cathedral City, CA 92234-3690

Uncle Bear Publishing is a trademark of Uncle Bear Publishing LLC.

Cover image: Jan Willis
Chapter art: Margaret Bodle
Cover and page design: Kevin Hile
Interior photos courtesy Jim Willis

ISBNs
Paperback: 979-8-9858304-2-2
EPub: 979-8-9858304-3-9
Audiobook: 979-8-9858304-4-6

Library of Congress Control Number: 2023936153

Printed in the United States of America.

Cosmo and Me

A Seeker's Journey from Religion to Spirituality

Jim Willis

www.UncleBearPublishing.com

About the Author

Theologian, historian, and musician Jim Willis earned his bachelor's degree from the Eastman School of Music and his master's degree from Andover Newton Theological School. An ordained minister for over 40 years, he served as an adjunct college professor and guest lecturer in comparative religion, cross-cultural studies, and contemporary spirituality. His background led to his writing more than 20 books on religion, the apocalypse, spirituality, and arcane or buried cultures, specializing in research bridging lost civilizations, suppressed history, and the study of earth energy, dowsing, and out-of-body experiences.

Contents

Cosmo and Me

Gather ye Rose-buds while ye may,
 Old Time is still a-flying:
And this same flower that smiles today,
 Tomorrow will be dying.

The glorious Lamp of Heaven, the Sun,
 The higher he's a getting;
The sooner will his Race be run,
 And nearer he's to Setting.

That Age is best, which is the first,
 When Youth and Blood are warmer;
But being spent, the worse, and worst
 Times, still succeed the former.

Then be not coy, but use your time;
 And while ye may, go marry:
For having lost but once your prime,
 You may forever tarry.

—Robert Herrick

Cosmo and Me

Preface

I'm one of the world's oldest Baby Boomers. Being born on April Fool's Day in 1946, the first year of the boom, gives me a certain seniority. I am now, for better or worse, an elder. Not that anyone cares. And not that it really matters, either. What's important is not how long you've lived, but what you've learned along the way. That's what makes an elder. Sad to say, for lo, these many years I've been doing what we all do—just getting along from day to day and not paying a whole lot of attention. Until lately.

I once wrote about the art of taking a long-distance bicycle journey in which I advised readers: "First, gather the flowers. Make sure you get a full array of colors. You can arrange them in a beautiful display later, after you have time to see how they fit together and highlight each other. That's what journeys are for—to gather the flowers of experience."

I have now come to believe that one of the purposes of eldership is to arrange the flowers you've picked up on your life's journey. And for those of us who have lived through the last seven decades, what a variety of colors we have gathered! But what makes my particular journey unique is that it has been specifically spent in a search for meaning—a quest, if you will, for the Holy Grail.

Now, an outlandish statement like that requires an explanation. In mythology, the Grail was an actual, physical object. It was tangible, not a collection of ideas. When Galahad and Percival set off on their quests, they weren't searching for a faith statement or a better way to explain God. They weren't even looking for something to believe in. They already believed. They were looking for something they could hold—something they could see and feel. It was hidden from the sight of most folks. Only those who took the time to look, who really translated their faith into action, who were willing to sweat and even suffer a little, were going to be able to achieve such a quest. Of course, it helped to have a pure heart—no easy feat!

In the America in which I began my quest, religion was mostly about saying publicly that you accepted a set of doctrines. As long as you stayed pretty close to orthodoxy, or at least didn't admit that you were a closet maverick, you were home free. You could join a church or synagogue (there were plenty to choose from), feast at the potluck suppers, pay your dues, and attend enough gatherings to keep the membership happy. It helped if you insulated yourself from embarrassing personal expressions. This was accomplished by referring to God as "the Man upstairs" or some such thing. You didn't pray, you "hit your knees" or asked for "a moment of silence." That kept you from making religion too personal. If you did all that, you were pretty well covered.

(I once was the final candidate to be the pastor of a small church that held my final interview in the church hall, attended by about a dozen people. When they were finished grilling me on my beliefs they asked if I had any questions for them. I asked what they talked about when the subject of God came up. After an embarrassing pause the spokeswoman said, "Well, that's something we don't talk about very much!" And this, you will remember, was a church group.)

I wanted more than that. For me, spirituality, a word I prefer over "religion," has always been about something real and tangible. I wanted to experience God. Notice the word "experience." I'm not talking about "knowing about," "studying," or "reading up on." To me, if God is real, then spiritual peek-a-boo just won't cut it. I see no sense in a God who created humans "in His image" and then left them to fend for themselves without any visible, or even invisible, means of support.

It sounds funny for a minister to say this, but because of my passion—sometimes I've even been forced to call it an obsession—religion has never been really satisfying for me. God was only exciting when I was learning something new, and I never found one way of thinking or practicing religion that explained and neatly codified all that could be known about God. I've run the gamut. After a full-blown fundamentalist conversion, I served time as an Evangelical, a Charismatic, a mainline conservative, and a flaming liberal. I've studied Zen Buddhism, Hinduism, Daoism, various Indian religions, philosophy, and New Age spiritualities. I've meditated, mediated, illuminated, contemplated, and postulated. I've taught more seminars than I can possibly remember, written books, and been a college professor, teaching courses in the fields of comparative religion and cross-cultural studies, as well as instrumental music. I've preached more than six thousand sermons, led Bible studies, and hosted a drive-time radio program called the *Through the Bible Series.*

After all this you would think a person like me would have the sense to call himself an expert and retire into a life of contentment and pleasure, but it didn't work that way. I never intended to give God a rest. Like Jacob of old, I wrestled with God my whole life, saying, "I will not let you go until you bless me!" I wasn't seeking some hope based on prayer and coincidence or a reasoned explanation about why we must "live by faith and not by sight." I wanted to experience the Holy. If God could condescend to speak to Abraham, Jacob, and Isaac, I figured He ought to be able to talk to me as well.

What this means is that all my life I wanted to experience a passion strong enough to inspire me to search for something tangible—the Holy Grail, if you will. When I retired, I figured I was old enough, stubborn enough, learned enough, experienced enough, and prickly enough to stop listening to the "experts" who are, by now, mostly younger than me and, in some cases, even my former students. To put it bluntly, I went looking for the meaning of life.

Although Boomers have been high on meaning ever since the beat generation gave way to the hippies, and although they have searched high and low along the byways of spirituality, most of my search has been within the protected confines of the Protestant church. In 2009 I retired as a pastor, having also put in a lot of part-time work as a carpenter, musician, public school teacher, college professor, and writer. And at long last I can say that my lifelong quest seems to have finally born fruit here in the woods of South Carolina. Having spent my years preaching and teaching *about* the Holy, I have finally *experienced* the Holy. And I found it right where it's always been—in our connection to nature and the very energy of the earth. My daughter was once asked, "What type of minister is your dad?" She thought for a moment and then said, "He's a Buddhist Christian who worships in the Native American tradition."

Make no mistake. I'm still a Christian, even though I haven't been inside a church for more than a decade. Christianity is still my home. But as a professor of world religions, I learned that Truth is a multifaceted gem. The discovery of that Truth, and the energy behind it, is the story of this book.

Some of my friends used to build houses. Others led big churches, played in major symphony orchestras, and taught at important colleges. A few collected food stamps. They were black and white, Asian and Latino, men and women, gay and straight, workers and retirees. They practiced Yoga, taught how to have Out of Body experiences, and wrote about metaphysics. Some swore either *by* or *at* both Deepak Chopra and Billy Graham. They were, indeed, a mixed bag. I seem to have gathered a multi-hued bouquet of flowers, so it's time to arrange them. Here goes.

Introduction:
The Search for the Holy Grail

Only the great ones, like old Charlie Dickens, can sum up an epoch, condense it to the size of a bumper sticker, and give it universal appeal. We all learned one of his best lines when we were in the ninth grade: "It was the best of times; it was the worst of times...." Perhaps that is all we know on Earth, and all we need to know.

That being said, however, you know you're getting old when you recall the idealistic, suburban, upwardly mobile, grass-covered, carefree neighborhood of your impressionistic youth and then realize you're talking about Detroit. We played football in the street, built tree forts, and went trick-or-treating without parents. We played baseball every Saturday morning and rode our bikes for miles out into the country without our moms ever asking where we'd been. The press manager for the Detroit Tigers lived right across the street, and his daughter was my on-again, off-again girlfriend, probably, I suppose, depending on what season of the year it was.

What shocks me most now is to look at old yearbooks and read the activities listed beneath the geeky pictures. There are the usual football, basketball, cheer-leading, and student council ones. But interspersed among them are entries such as "youth fellowship" and "choir." Those aren't school-related activities. They were church groups. Impossible as it sounds to folks today, it seemed as if everyone went to church, at least occasionally, in the 1950s.

I did, to the point where I can't remember anyone who sang in our church choir who didn't also sing in the school glee club.

Those were the heady days when young men had come marching home victorious from the last righteous war. Flush with talent produced with help from the GI Bill and plentiful money from war-time contracts, industry went into overdrive. The American suburb was invented. Churches started to build "Fellowship Halls" and become the center of polite society.

And so it happened that it was in a church that I faced down my greatest fear and experienced the moment that probably changed my life. The situation had nothing to do with salvation or some equally prosaic future event. No, it was much more immediate.

In 1958 about 15 clean-scrubbed, tan-khakied, oxford-shirted, white-socked, and black-loafered 12-year-olds sat around an Elmer's glue-sticky table, the end result of a confirmation class sponsored by a big Presbyterian church in downtown Detroit. By now we had learned the books of the Bible, the 23rd Psalm, the "chief end of man," and other essentials that would be needed on the road to salvation, adulthood, and other great mysteries of life. We had performed our community service and passed muster before the board of deacons or whatever they were called back then. Now there was just one more hurdle on the road between us and the pearly gates. We waited for the assistant minister to call our names and ask what we wanted to be when we grew up.

For me it was worse than for everyone else. We had been told what was coming and had all prepared a heartfelt, sure-to-be-inspiring rendition of what our teachers had told us to say. That was the easy part.

But I stuttered. Badly. I couldn't get two words out of my mouth before looking and sounding like a stranded fish out of water. Sure enough, right on schedule, fear set in and terror gripped my very soul. My last name began with a W. I was near the end. I had plenty of time to develop a good panic. To this day I cannot remember how the Brown and Collins kids planned to spend the rest of their lives. You'd think I would have been used to the tension by then, after all those embarrassing moments spent in classrooms up and down the hallways of our institutionally brown-painted, three-floored schools that we "entered to learn" so that we might "go

"I-I---I w-w-w-want t-t-t-t-to be a p-p-p-preacher."
—Jimmy Willis (early 1950s)

forth to serve." Our teachers were preparing us for great things in the "best of times" to come. But my speech impediment was something I never could get around, over, or through. A stutterer in the golden age of conformity stood out like a black tick on a white dog.

The tension grew to a fever pitch until finally I heard my name and was asked to stand and tell the class about my great ambition—the Purpose that would consume my life to come.

"I-I—I w-w-w-want t-t-t-t-to be a p-p-p-preacher," I said.

A future stand-up comedian couldn't have brought the house down more than I did that day long ago. But in the midst of all the laughter there was one person who was moved to tears of a different sort. I had, for the first time in my young life, given voice to something I considered worth living for and thus managed to express my intention out loud.

And wonder of wonders, "it came to pass," as the familiar words of the Good Book so often say. That's exactly what happened. I became a preacher, and a successful one, if the many

Cosmo and Me

thank-you letters and phone calls over the years mean anything. Now, in my retirement, I have finally learned that reality moves at a much slower pace than that which we Boomers have grown to espouse. To find it we have to slow down. Way, way down, I have discovered. And the act of slowing down is much harder than you would expect. The words taught to me as a kid in the church of my youth are now, much to my surprise, beginning to make sense. "Fear not … Peace … Now is the day … Love one another."

So here in the last act of my life's drama, surrounded by Gaia herself and a forest full of mystery and meaning, I think I've finally reached the end of my quest. I've found my Holy Grail. Only *you* know where *your* Grail is hidden. But perhaps, as we journey together, we can find the way. Let's begin at the beginning.

Chapter 1:
The Age of the Hero (the 1950s)

THE CULTURE

From Flash Gordon to Zorro by way of Davy Crockett. Who was Joe McCarthy? We didn't know. He never had his own TV show. We never understood the Korean War either until our third time through the M*A*S*H* reruns many years later. As a kid I made music with Maestro Valter Poole of the Detroit Symphony while hobnobbing with Al Kaline of the Detroit Tigers major league baseball team, and somehow, I took it all for granted. Spirituality in the '50s took the shape of Leave it to Beaver and Donna Reed. It was institutional. The big difference between Fundamentalist and Liberal churches was ideology. Socially, they followed the same practices. From conservative Billy Graham to liberal Norman Vincent Peale, it was a time of heroes.

Picture, in your mind's eye, a placid pond or small lake on a beautiful summer day. The sky overhead is broken only by an occasional white puffy cloud that serves to accentuate, rather than diminish, the beauty of deep blue and golden sunshine sparkling on the water before you. The calm and quiet surface of the lake is broken only by the ripples that spread out from the actions of a few quiet ducks, or maybe even a loon or two. Once or twice a fish rises to the top to slurp up an unseen insect, but the overall impression is one of peace and tranquility.

If you were to don a mask and make use of a snorkeling tube, however, peering beneath the surface, you would see quite a different world. Survival of the fittest is the name of the game down there. Big fish eat small fish. Innocent bugs, living out their brief lives, become meals for frogs. Clean sand gives rise to weeds and slimy plants that soon turn the bottom into muck and ooze that will suck you down if you try to walk across the shallows. In direct contrast to the placid surface, it is not a pleasant place at all, although it certainly harbors a lot of life.

Once in a while a storm blows out of the north. The smooth water is pelted with rain and wind, forcing anyone who ventures out to return to port and take shelter inside. But with the passing of the storm, peace returns, leaving only a vague memory of turmoil and unpleasantness.

In my mind, that image is a perfect metaphor for the America of my youth. In 1950 I turned four years old. I was raised in the upper-middle class, white, manicured neighborhoods of the suburbs. It was certainly, on the surface at least, an ideal way to grow up. Everything glittered. Beneath the surface pulsed a whole world of racism and inequality that a young kid such as myself never glimpsed. Once in a while it surfaced when the "N" word was uttered or adults spoke about subjects that went way over our heads. To this day I can't understand why we never considered it strange to be taught how to duck and cover under our desks. We were sure that if the evil empire ever attacked, they would first bomb Grand Rapids, Michigan. But somehow, after the drill was over, we just went home and played Cowboys and Indians or made what we called "set-ups" with our GI Joe action figures. We simply did not equate war drills with reality. The outside world just didn't exist.

Unless, of course, you count the music of Elvis Presley. The hair, the shoes, the hips, the guitar, the beat — it was intoxicating. And our parents hated it! What more could you ask? By this time, we had all become accustomed to TV sets, but suddenly transistor radios were all the rage. No more plugging in! We could take them with us wherever we went. Free at last! Free at last. Thank God Almighty, we were free at least!

In hindsight, though, Elvis had a lot of help. Just when we discovered *him* around about 1956, marketing companies discovered *us*. We had money to spend. It was the beginning of a generations-long love affair between Madison Avenue and teenagers. Elvis was soon everywhere, providing the first soundtrack of the Baby Boom generation.

Add all this together while Cadillacs and Chevys got bigger tail fins every year and what do you get? "The best of times and the worst of times."

I experienced most of this decade while living in Detroit, Michigan, and what I remember most vividly was Flash Gordon, Davy Crockett, and Zorro. There were hula hoops, as well, and various fads such as stilts, roller skates that you tightened to your shoes with a key, shuffleboards and, for some reason, spool knitting. But mostly I seem to remember having a lot of fun while the world suffered through its tragedies. I guess that's what happens when you're young, white, middle class, lucky, and ignorant.

I have one memory from that decade, however, that still haunts me today. I hope confession is good for the soul.

Most people trace the economic downturn--"collapse" might be a better word--of the present state of affairs in Detroit to the race riots and "white flight" that occurred in 1967. I know better.

Detroit's woes began in the summer of 1956, and I helped start the ball rolling. I won't say it was all my fault, but Victor Gruen and Dwight Eisenhower and the ghost of Henry Ford and I got together around then to concoct the perfect storm that is now raging. So, at the risk of sounding a bit Forest Gumpish, this is . . .

HOW I PRECIPITATED THE DOWNFALL OF DETROIT (WITH A LITTLE HELP FROM MY FRIENDS)

The Northland Center Shopping Mall on Greenfield Road in Southfield, a suburb of Detroit, was the brainchild of a far-seeing marketing/engineering genius named Victor Gruen. He had a vision of surrounding Detroit with a string of shopping malls, one located at each of the four compass points surrounding the city.

They would be "way out" in the suburbs, and many people thought he was crazy, but Hudson's Department Store took a chance on him. Remember, now, that this was an American prototype. There were no shopping malls like this in the country yet. The idea of spending $30,000,000 dollars to build some stores that nobody could walk to was insane, but when Hudson's grossed $88,000,000 in their first year, people began to come around.

Northland was the talk of the country. The *Wall Street Journal* featured it in a prominent article. It was written up in *Time, Look, Life, Newsweek* and, of course, the *Ladies Home Journal.* All these magazines heralded Northland as the coming thing, the first and largest big-time shopping mall in the country — an example for all to follow.

Nowadays it looks a lot different. It's under cover, for one thing. Back then you still had to carry an umbrella on rainy days. The store names have changed, of course. Hudson's merged with Dayton's of Minneapolis and then morphed into what we now know as *Target,* for instance. But it featured banks and a post office. There were fountains, statues, supermarkets, and a center for lost children. (I always confused this with Pater Pan's *Neverland.*) They even gave you free gasoline if you ran out in the parking lot. Really! They did! Free gas!

Later in life, Victor Gruen grew to hate what he had unleashed on the world. In a 1978 interview, as reported by M. Jeffrey Hardwick in his 2010 book, *Mall Maker,* Gruen railed against the ugly, mercenary approach to life that his creation had made possible. "I refuse to pay alimony for those bastard developments," he said. But by then it was too late. The damage had been done. America had entered a new phase.

What does all this have to do with the downfall of Detroit? Hang on. Now it starts to get complicated.

What made Victor's idea work was that he foresaw something others didn't. In 1956 President Eisenhower passed a highway act that proposed building more than 41,000 miles of interstate highways. The Ford Motor Company, based in Detroit, had lobbied heavily for this act, and how do you say no to both Henry Ford and the General who won the war? The idea was that such an infrastructure would protect the country in case another war broke out. It would make it easier to get supplies from coast to coast and everywhere in between.

But no one was fooled by this. Then as now, big corporations--specifically, those that made cars--had an ulterior motive. As far as a highly efficient interstate highway system was concerned, they knew that if the federal government built it, people would use it. "If you build it, they will come." Which simply means people would be moved to buy more cars.

But this created another side benefit. People didn't have to live in close proximity to work anymore. Why live in a crowded, dirty city when you could move out to the suburbs and commute to work? The roads were soon to be in place. Detroit could certainly supply the cars. A lot of construction companies would give a lot of people labor-type jobs. Voilà! Suburbia was born. And as people moved out of town, Victor Gruen's masterpiece was waiting for them. There stood Northland, ready and waiting with a huge parking lot. One stop shopping. As a matter of fact, it was much more than shopping. It was an experience of socializing with friends, eating out, getting away from the house, leaving town, and living the life of the rich, or at least the middle class.

Pretty soon everything moved out of town. And the people followed. Look at the figures. In 1950, when the first Boomers were four years old, 1.8 million people lived in Detroit. By 1960 the population had dropped by 10 percent. During the same time period, the suburbs, now called the Metro Detroit Region, grew by 25 percent. And who were these people who moved to the suburbs? They were primarily Big 3 auto workers, who received high wages and great benefits because they belonged to a strong, politically connected union. They made their money in the city and spent it in the suburbs. Eventually, the auto plants moved to the suburbs, too. What happened to the tax base in the inner city? It declined, of course. The home with the dog and the picket fence was now the base for the American Dream. "It was the best of times!"

Those who say Detroit's problems began with "white flight" after the race riots of 1967 have simply not done their homework. The central fact is this: when auto workers left for greener pastures, they took their money with them. Corruption in government, "sweetheart deals," and union shenanigans didn't help, of course, but they were not the underlying cause of the problem. When it comes to suburbia, the barbeque rules!

Dinah Shore's siren song rang throughout the nation: "See the USA in your Chevrolet!" And America responded like lemmings. They headed for the open highway. Gas was cheap. The Shah of Iran made sure of that. The highways were free. The government made sure of that. Cars were plentiful. Ford, General Motors, and Chrysler made sure of that. The horizon beckoned. And off we went. We were on our way to cup holders in every minivan, soccer moms, and the morning commute. Dunkin' Donuts, McDonald's, and the "drive-through window" beckoned us. Obesity was right around the corner. The seats in Tiger Stadium soon had to be built a lot wider than they had been.

But wait a minute. I said I had something to do with all this. What part did I play? It happened like this....

In the summer of 1956, I was 10 years old. That's a good age. It's old enough to have the illusion of freedom but not too old to have to face the problems associated with the actual experience of it. I had a friend that year, Mike, who walked to school with me and generally shared my love of plastic soldiers, pirate fantasies, and Lone Ranger toy six-guns. (The famous Mattel "Fanner Fifty" was still a few years away, but by golly we were close!)

Summers must have been tough on moms back then. The family cultural model was in rapid flux. Before we were born, children were seen as being, for all intents and purposes, labor-saving devices. They were made to work in the fields, along with Dad and Grandpa, and support their parents when old age finally caught up to them. Beginning with us, and continuing even today, children ruled. They are now the ones in charge, and families have to pretty much accommodate them or run the risk of, at best, addling their children for life or, at worst, being guilty of child abuse.

Parents didn't know that back then. Psychiatric therapy was still rare. As Tom Eagleton learned in 1972, when George McGovern tapped him for the vice-presidential spot, a trip to a psychiatrist, even for the best of reasons, was seen back then as a sign of instability, so parents didn't yet know how easy it was to scar their kids for life.

But all this was still in the future. We were the in-between generation. We had chores to do. Perhaps we were no longer sentenced to a summer's incarceration of weeding endless miles of corn and potatoes, but we had to at least mow the lawn and paint the picket fence. When we were done, though, we were free! If only to get us *out* of the house, our mothers, who still worked *in* the house, told us to go outside and play.

And did we ever! Einstein was right about time being relative. Those were the days when the hours between 12:00 lunch and 6:00 dinner took about a week and a half. But we were still around, and our mothers were still chained to the house in case anything went wrong. It must have seemed like a miracle from Heaven, therefore, when Mike came up with the featured idea of the summer. His father was a carpenter and was working on the expansion of Northland Mall. Would I like to go with him to work for a day or so?

Would I? You're kidding! It was a win/win for everyone. Mike and I got to go on an adventure, the moms were free for the day, and the dads didn't care as long as we stayed out of trouble. It was perfect! I couldn't believe my luck. I was supposed to paint the fence that summer, and now I was, at least temporarily, reprieved!

The fateful day finally arrived. I don't remember how and why the construction supervisors allowed such a thing. I don't remember much of what we did that day. I now suspect that Mike was going to have to, for whatever reason, go with his dad that day anyway, and I was brought along to keep him out of trouble. But one moment stands out in vivid detail. Mike's dad was building finished shelves in what was to be a shoe store. No one had pneumatic nail guns in those days. Every nail was pounded in by hand. A carpenter would take a finish nail out of their mouth (I swear that carpenters in those days could eat lunch without removing a whole mouthful of nails), tap it once, and then with one blow, sometimes two, they would seat the nail all the way to the head. Way before "wax on, wax off!" This was magic! For some reason, I had to learn how to do it.

And Mike's dad was only too happy to show me, probably because I was doing his work for him. (To this day I wonder if I should bill Northland for back pay.) Mike soon got sick of it and went off to cause trouble on his own, but I was on my way to becoming a carpenter. I was in "the trades!" I was building a bright, future America. I don't know if a string section really started playing background music, but I'm fairly sure the angels sang. It was one of those days when the endless movie of summer turned into a Technicolor slideshow frozen in time. Ever since that day, I have been, at least in my heart, a carpenter.

What would have happened if I hadn't been there to help? Would the shoe store have remained unfinished? Would Northland have caved? Would people never have started moving to the suburbs? Whatever might have happened, I must bear the guilt of helping Victor Gruen fulfill his dream while becoming the unwitting pawn of both the Ford Motor Company's and the Eisenhower administration's cynical plot to sell more cars. This would lead to global pollution, urban blight, the oil embargo of 1973, and a host of other tragedies, eventually leading to the present woes of Detroit, that jewel of a city where little boys once played and dreamed of greater things.

It wasn't all work, though. We played a lot and sometimes learned lessons that have stood the test of time. When I was young, a big group of us used to get together every Saturday morning to play baseball at a local park. Those were the days before adults supervised kids' activities so much. I guess we must have had Little League and organized sports, but none of us ever participated. We used to choose our own teams and make up our own rules.

The younger kids tried hard to belong, and the older ones practiced the skills they would someday need in middle management. There was a definite pecking order, and it used to seem terribly important to know where you stood, a place determined by how soon you were chosen and what position you were told to play. The person who was chosen last always played right field and never talked much. It was an exercise in playground dynamics and only the ones who were in charge really enjoyed it.

I never thought about it much. I just went along like everybody else. It was simply what you did on Saturday mornings back in our neighborhood.

But one day when I was in seventh or eighth grade, a revolution took place. A guy named Mike—not that Mike, another one, I've forgotten his last name—had recently moved into our neighbor-hood. (Kids today are all named "Dude." Back then it was "Mike.") This Mike was an independent type, maybe even the world's first flower child. He was a good baseball player, soon moving to the top of the pecking order. But maybe because he was a new kid, or maybe, as I like to think, because he was a free thinker, he hadn't really become one of the playground CEOs who ran things. He was a maverick, apt to befriend the younger kids who played right field, that sort of thing.

One day a rules dispute broke out. I seem to remember that somebody forgot to tag up on the rock that was third base and ran home before a fly ball was caught out in center field. Maybe it was something else. Memory can be tricky. All I know for sure is that, since I wasn't directly involved, not really caring whether we won or lost, probably not even knowing what the score was, I just waited for the argument to be settled.

I was standing next to Mike, who was also watching the whole thing transpire, and remember him looking over at me and saying, "This isn't much fun. Let's go home and do something else."

Go home? You mean I can just do that? Don't I have to stay here and finish the game? Isn't that what everyone does around here?

We didn't say anything else. We didn't discuss what was about to become a playground revolution. Not really understanding it was a moment of destiny, we just picked up our gloves and left.

"Where're you going?" was the demand from our team captain. It was uttered in roughly the same tone of voice a prison guard might use if an inmate headed out the front gate. Alone, I probably would have either meekly returned to my position at second base or at least muttered some excuse about my mother calling me. But Mike didn't even hesitate.

"This is a waste of time," he said for all to hear. "We're leaving."

Such blasphemy, such world-shattering words of revolution, had never before been declared in the remembered history of our little society. Someone had dared utter the truth most of us felt but never dared speak out loud.

Once said, those words took on a life of their own. A mighty chorus began to swell from all over the diamond, even from right field. Tired of the few bossing the many, the voices of the downtrodden were heard. The powerful idea that Saturday mornings were supposed to be fun struggled forth into the light of day and burst into glorious flower.

To this day I can vividly see the faces of the playground bullies. Open disbelief. They simply couldn't understand with their minds what their intuition grasped in that moment of horror. Their world had been turned upside down. The masses had revolted and found strength in numbers, all because someone dared voice what all knew to be true but had found neither words nor will to articulate. Things didn't have to be the way they were. They could be changed.

Who knows? Maybe the whole '60s revolution began right there on that Detroit playground on a Saturday morning in June.

This idealism raises an interesting question:

THE QUESTION

Can you develop a richly hued spirituality within the confines of a vanilla society?

With a background like mine, in which I have to really reach to claim any serious childhood difficulties or troubles to overcome, is it possible to develop a rich sense of spirituality?

To answer that question, we first have to define spirituality. In most dictionaries it comes down to something like this:

> *Spirituality is the quality of being concerned with the human spirit or soul as opposed to material or physical things.*

That's good, but it's only a start. Here are three more opinions:

- Christina Puchalski, MD, Director of the George Washington Institute for Spirituality and Health, contends that "spirituality is the aspect of humanity that refers to the way individuals seek and express meaning and purpose and the way they experience their connectedness to the moment, to self, to others, to nature, and to the significant or sacred."
- According to Mario Beauregard and Denyse O'Leary, researchers and authors of *The Spiritual Brain*, "spirituality means any experience that is thought to bring the experiencer into contact with the divine." In other words, not just any experience that feels meaningful.
- Ruth Beckmann Murray and Judith Proctor Zenter write that "the spiritual dimension tries to be in harmony with the universe, and strives for answers about the infinite, and comes into focus when the person faces emotional stress, physical illness, or death."

Better. But a bit wordy and high-falutin'.

My definition is a bit simpler. I define spirituality as that which seeks to help you experience the essential essence of reality (or perhaps I should say Reality, with a capitol "R"). I once tried to put into words in a book what I mean by this concept. It was self-published and is no longer in print, but it went like this:

> *When I retired to the woods, I wasn't exactly sure how to go about my task of experiencing the Holy. I mean, short of the angel Gabriel appearing with trumpet in hand, how can God actually communicate*

with you? You can get impressions while deep in prayer. You can have coincidences happen. Once, for instance, when I was really strapped for cash, I prayed for money and got a check in the mail the next day. Stuff like that happens, and for most people, I suppose, that's sufficient. But not for me. It's just too subjective. I wanted something I could see and touch.

There's also another problem. By the time I retired I had long given up on the concept of God that postulates a "Being" somehow separate and distinct from me. I don't picture God as an old man sitting on a cloud, watching with interest what goes on down here on planet Earth, perhaps even wringing "His" hands in worry and fret about the state of the human race. To me, God simply is not that personal. If that's what it takes for some people to try to wrap their minds around a concept of God, far be it from me to argue. But for me it just won't work. The only way I can think about God that makes sense is to think in terms of a cosmic, infinite Consciousness, an eternal Other that is beyond words and even ideas. This is a classic Hindu idea. Brahma, "God," is beyond language or even categories of thought. If you try to describe it, you have, by definition, fallen short.

What I'm saying, simply, is this: Human beings are spiritual beings. That is our reality. Spirituality is the art and craft of getting in touch with that which we already are but have forgotten in the course of our busy, hectic, material lives.

I have a fond memory from childhood that has stayed with me into adulthood. It is of my very first carpentry project.

I've already mentioned that I come from a church family. Christianity was the vehicle through which we attempted to interface with the Holy. We all sang in choirs, went to Sunday school, and attended church services. Missing church on a Sunday was not an option in our house. We might be too sick to go to school during the week, but to miss a Sunday morning meant someone was almost on their death bed. My grandmother was awarded a wonderful tribute before her passing, presented to her by members of the Sunday school class she taught for 50 years. It was a beautifully framed painting called *The Walk to Emmaus*, a picture of the famous post-resurrection appearance of Jesus, when he revealed himself to two unknown disciples on Easter morning. Alumni from her class, who call themselves the Grace Willis Sunday School Class, still meet once a year for a reunion. As a child, when I visited her at her house, she would sit in a rocking chair that now sits in my living room and read Bible stories to me from *The Children's Story Bible*, a volume that proudly graces my bookshelf to this day.

My father was the choir director at our church, and my mother was the organist. I sat with my grandmother during the interminable Sunday morning services and listened to her *sotto voce* responses to the minister's sermons. After church every Sunday we would go home to a dinner that usually featured roast sermon, at least in terms of family conversations.

On the altar of our church sanctuary stood a beautiful brass cross. It was mounted on a pedestal consisting of three graduated platforms, each smaller than the one below it. I think they probably symbolized the Trinity. When I was in third or fourth grade, I went down to my father's workshop one day and built a cross like that for myself. It was probably pretty crude, consisting of two narrow boards nailed together for a cross and three boards of descending size for the platform. But it was built with pride and devotion, and I placed it on a makeshift altar in my bedroom.

I don't know what happened to that cross, but I'd give a lot to have it today. It indicates to me that even at a very early age I was seeking a way to bring the holy down into my life, which makes me ponder the age-old nature/nurture debate. Was I, or, for that matter, were any of us, born with an innate spiritual tendency, or is that something we develop as we grow older?

I've thought about this a lot, and although I can't speak for anyone else's experience, in my case I think I must have been a born seeker. How could it be otherwise for one so young to strive to seek the face of God? Perhaps even my thirst for music was somehow an expression of this spiritual nature, although at the beginning I suspect music soon became a vehicle for self-confidence. I was only an average athlete and student, but I was a good musician.

Someone—and I can't track down who it was--once said that you can't be a good jazz musician unless you've experienced a painful childhood. I don't know if that's true or not. To tell you the truth, I don't know of anyone who *didn't* experience a painful childhood. But mine was certainly not painful compared to many of those to whom I've ministered and befriended over the years. I had three people close to me—two teacher/mentors and a family member—commit suicide while I was growing up. One did so in the 1950s, one in the '60s, and one in the '70s. Since then, because I was a minister, there have been others, of course. But those three marked the first three defining decades of my march to adulthood, so there must have been a lot going on under the surface during years that I remember as being very peaceful and unruffled. I just didn't know what it was. I do now, having experienced the tumultuous '60s and '70s, but I didn't back then.

So, in answer to my question, "Can you develop a richly hued spirituality within the confines of a vanilla society?" I guess the answer is, "Yes, but it may take a lifetime to express itself in a way that is meaningful." At least, that has been my experience.

That brings up another observation that is best expressed by a second question: "Are religion and spirituality the same thing?"

I don't know what others might say. Language is notoriously subjective, despite what we are taught in school. But, again in my experience, no they are not. As I just pointed out, to me, spirituality is about experiencing the essence of Reality. Having finally attained my senior years, I'm not even comfortable using the word "God" in public anymore. Too many people have definitions for that word that are nowhere near what I mean when I say it. Personally, I like the word "God." I even still consider myself a Christian, even though I rarely define myself that way to others and I'm certain many of my old Christian friends would say I have left the path.

In my humble opinion, however thinking and feeling humans arrived on the scene, however life came about, however our particular species rose to the damaging heights we now occupy, whatever God or Source or Force was behind it, even if that God/Source/Force someday proves to be completely secular or scientific rather than metaphysical or supernatural, the process invokes spirituality.

But spirituality, especially when felt at an intuitive level by a child, usually finds its first expression within an organizational framework. That means, most often, a religion of some kind.

Christianity is my home, the place where I am most comfortable. True, I consider the dogmas and doctrines to be outmoded and insufficient, sometimes even harmful. But I still find that the religion I have practiced my whole life contains the best set of metaphors for explaining the essence of reality. I'm constantly surprised at new ways I now understand old truths. Oh—and I love the music.

Religion, to my mind, is an earthly infrastructure for spirituality. Kids need boundaries. Religion supplies them. Thus, it is an important discipline, even if it serves only to give a young adult something to push off from when he or she feels its yoke to be too constraining.

But remember this. It is only an infrastructure. And not, by any means, the only one. Religion is one expression, one manifestation, of spirituality, but it is often flawed and seldom representative of the spiritual experience of the original founder or founders. A lot of people who follow a particular religion are not spiritual. Many are not even close.

Once in a while, however, it works. Some aura of spirituality must have been present to move a young boy to build a cross out of wood and create a makeshift altar in his bedroom. That's important to remember. That same aura must have drawn him back every week, and later convinced him to become a minister. Parents can compel church attendance. They cannot compel a vocation in ministry. That comes from somewhere else.

Where? I'm tempted to think it comes most often through the example of a hero. Usually an elder hero. Often a professional one. Sometimes a long line of them.

Let me explain.

As a kid I loved to play sports. All sports. All the time. Earlier I mentioned that my girlfriend was the daughter of the press manag-

I loved to play sports. All sports. All the time. Soccer at Interlochen National Music Camp (1963).

er for the Detroit Tigers. Once in a while I got good tickets, sometimes right behind the third base dugout. My favorite player was the great Al Kaline. Once I even got a baseball that he may or may not have hit into the stands during batting practice. My girlfriend's father implied that he had been the one who hit it, but the fact that Kaline was my favorite player might have influenced the story.

At any rate, I was hooked on baseball, and my dad and I once made a last-minute decision to go to a late-afternoon game during those glorious days when ball clubs played day games, there were seats almost always available, and tickets were affordable. I'll never forget that day for two reasons. The first was that we sat out in right field in the first row of seats, right over the head of Al Kaline. At one point during the game, he chased a ball into the hole, caught up with it right underneath where we were sitting, no more than 20 feet from us, and threw out a runner who was trying to score from second base. He got him by three feet, and I had a chance to see exactly how far it was from the right field fence to home plate. If I had tried to make that throw, I wouldn't have even reached second base without a lot of bounces. We didn't have zip codes back in those days, but if we did, I'm sure right field and home plate would have had different numbers. I'm not sure they were even in the same time zone. To say I was in awe would be an understatement. Al Kaline was, and still is, a hero of mine.

But the second reason I remember that day is because of something unrelated to baseball. In those days, ball clubs used to do all kinds of things to entertain the fans. On this day, they had a small Dixieland band playing in the stands, roaming around wherever two or more folks were gathered together. They came over and played a tune for us. I was enchanted. I had never before heard music like this live. They were really good, but I was even more impressed when the bass drum player yelled out, "Hey, Lyle!" to my father. Apparently, they knew each other. I had no idea. He became another hero of sorts, and, to tell you the truth, my dad grew a little taller that day as well. It never occurred to me that he had a life and might know people outside our family circle. I mean, I knew he left home every day to go work at a job somewhere, but I didn't know where he went or what he did. All I knew was that the company he worked for had the authority to call him every three or four years and tell him to move to a new city. So far, we had lived in Grand Rapids, Detroit, Chicago, and then back to Detroit. By the time I was in the seventh grade, I had experienced four towns, four schools, and four new sets of friends. To tell you the truth, I still hate big oil companies. (Of course, at this stage of my life I have a lot more reasons to do so.)

Although I liked sports, I was never a really great athlete. Good, maybe, but not great. Where I excelled was music. I can say it honestly because I have the evidence to back it up, but I was a really good trombone player. That was why, shortly after the experience at the ballpark, I got a chance to play in my first professional symphony orchestra.

The church we attended had a superb music program. It featured two complete 40-voice choirs (one for each Sunday morning service), professional soloists, a full-time organist or two, and about four or five children's choirs. The music director was another hero of mine. George Thomas had about as much to do with my love of church music as anyone, and I will forever remember him with reverence. When he retired to Arizona, I was able to

I was a really good trombone player. National Youth Symphony (1964).

contact him during one of my cross-country bike trips. He lived in a rest home that turned out to be his final home on earth. He was surprised when I showed up but remembered those days with as much fondness as I did. I consider it a great blessing that, as an adult, I could tell him how much he meant to me before he died.

The church choirs combined to perform two major Oratorios every year--one at Christmas time and another around Easter--with full orchestral accompaniment. This year the offering was the Verde *Requiem*. For those not familiar with this piece, it is a tour de force that makes brass players salivate whenever they know they will get to play it.

The orchestra thus featured a full brass section but needed a second trombone player. My dad played first trombone. He had a symphonic background, having led the trombone section and been the concert manager of the Grand Rapids Symphony for years. He was also, up to this point, the only teacher I ever had. He must have thought I was ready. Having heard the recording we made; I agree. I was good, even though I was only 12 years old.

I practiced my head off because the conductor of the performance was Dr. Valter Poole, who at that time was one of the conductors of the Detroit Symphony. This was my first opportunity to play with the big boys, and I wanted everything to be perfect.

Come the day of the first rehearsal, I was in place early, as was the entire orchestra. The only one missing was the percussionist. Percussion, especially tympani and bass drum, were really important in this piece. Where was he? Didn't he know this was a professional gig?

Just before we began, the back doors of the concert hall opened up and in walked the percussionist, carrying a big bass drum. To my horror, it was the guy who played bass drum in the Dixieland band at Tiger Stadium! He walked slowly up the center aisle, and I was terrified that the great Dr. Poole would walk off the podium in a well-deserved huff. To think we were wasting time with a guy who played at ballparks!

When the drummer got right below the podium where the maestro stood, he looked up and said, "Hi, Walt!"

Dr. Poole responded, "Hi, Dick!"

I later learned that my Dixieland drummer hero was also the principal percussionist of the Detroit Symphony. Who knew you could play the music of both Louis Armstrong and Giuseppe Verde on the same drum?

The rest of that day is a blur. But something wonderful happened. For the first time, I experienced that holy feeling of playing real music with real musicians. The fact that it was liturgical music probably helped a lot. When you are surrounded by top-flight artists, playing music written for the church, and then couple that with the fact that you are surrounded by a sense of holiness never before experienced by a 12-year-old kid not yet jaded by the business of music, it can change your life. Indeed, it did change my life. I've conducted a lot of really good choirs and orchestras and played with some world-class musicians since then, but nothing has quite compared to that initial performance. I guess that was the day I lost my musical virginity. Nevertheless, for me, that kind of music has always been a spiritual experience. It was there that I first heard the voice of angels and perhaps even saw the face of God.

It all came about because of a string of heroes: my father, George Thomas, Al Kaline, Maestro Poole, and a drummer whose last name I have forgotten. Through such people, none of whom ever realized the part they played, spirituality grew and shaped my life.

Was it luck? Was it serendipity? Was it coincidence? Was it God? To this day, I still don't know. But that experience has taught me something that I have chosen to believe, whether it is true or not. I have come to believe that each one of us has a responsibility to take whatever cards we have been dealt and play the game with gusto.

That's very easy to say. It sounds like a platitude. Maybe it even is one. But platitudes are plentiful because they express a universal truth. We cannot choose our parents, or the circumstances into which we are born. But the moment we decide to take over the reins of our own life and live authentically, entering into what we feel is our own destiny, is the very same moment we move from childhood into the world of spiritual adulthood.

The Bible says it simply but elegantly: "Choose you this day whom you will serve." No one else can make the choice for us. The great mythologist Joe Campbell used to say, "Follow your bliss." It's the same thing. The brass ring does not discriminate. It is available for all to grab.

Alas, some never do. They are afraid to lose their grip on the Merry-Go-'Round of life and reach for their destiny.

Maybe that's the essence of spirituality. It is the force that compels us toward our destiny, the purpose of our existence, the reason we were born. It forces us to let go, to leave our comfort zone and consider greater possibilities, to reach for that Something That Is Greater Than Ourselves.

If a child who came of age in the 1950s, a child of privilege who was raised in a vanilla-flavored culture, can spend the last years of his life seeking an experience of Reality, it must have been an important decade.

Was there an undercurrent that I felt but couldn't quite explain? There must have been. Another hero of mine represents exhibit A of that theory.

My beloved shop teacher, the one who was the single greatest influence on my career as a carpenter, the one who I most wanted to emulate and who might have even drawn me away from a career in music and directed me toward industrial arts, decided one day, for reasons that I cannot even begin to comprehend, to pick up a deer rifle, walked out into a vacant lot, and put a bullet through his head.

I heard about it just before the decade concluded. It upended everything I thought I knew about life. It pulled the spiritual rug out from under my feet that had, until this time, provided a secure and stable resting place. It made me confront death for the first time.

I still have on my bookshelves two books on carpentry that my shop teacher, Ira Madden, wrote. He was one of the only reasons I ever wanted to go to school in the morning. Shop class was one of the few bright spots in an otherwise hated educational process. And now he was no more.

His death was the first real unsettling experience in my life. But it was soon to be followed by many more. The '60s were about to unsettle a lot of people. Life in America was about to change forever.

And few of us saw it coming.

Cosmo and Me

Chapter 2:
The Cradle Shall Fall (the 1960s)

THE CULTURE

In the fall of 1960, I entered a practice room to learn how to be a professional trombonist. When I emerged, in the summer of '68, the world had changed. From psychedelics to Eastern religions, those who once sat next to me in church classes had been experimenting with things I never knew existed. But looming over it all was the dark, consuming shadow of Vietnam. When your draft lottery number is 33, idealism suddenly takes a back seat.

There is something to say for being young, idealistic, sheltered, and, let's call it like it is, self-centered. It's a comfortable existence.

In the school year 1959 to '60 I began to dwell in a different world. First, we moved from the Midwest to the East Coast—from Detroit to New York. That's about 500 miles as the crow flies, but light years apart in every other way.

First of all, it meant changing schools again, a fact for which I will be forever grateful. I absolutely hated the impersonal high school I was attending in Detroit, complete with teachers who showed up for the job but couldn't stand the students. I never liked school much at all, period. But I have no doubts that had I stayed on at Thomas M. Cooley High School on the corner of Hubbell Avenue and Chalfonte Street in Detroit's northwest side, I might never have graduated from High School at all. I'm sure that even though the school is now closed, there are some graduates

The leader of the band. Drum Major, Pleasantville High School Marching Band (1964).

who look back fondly at their years there. Both my sister and her husband did. I'm happy for them, but I'm happier for me that I got out.

It seems ironic to me that I escaped what I considered to be a terrible environment to spend the next four years of my life at a place called Pleasantville in Westchester County, a suburb of New York City.

Please understand, I didn't like school there, either, but it was made bearable because I made some good friends, all of whom liked music. And band was what made my life endurable.

I needed something to consume me during those times. A respected teacher, who had made me feel welcome in my new school and who did more than anyone to help me overcome my inadequacies when it came to mathematics, one day decided to commit suicide.

For the second time in my life, I was blindsided by the voluntary death of a mentor. I never knew why he did it. To this day, I don't know. All I can say, now that I have the blessing of experience and some amount of accumulated wisdom, is that perhaps whatever demons drove my mentors to take their own lives, they were mentors precisely because something within me spoke to that something that was within them. Deep calling onto deep. We never spoke about anything morbid. They were both upbeat and positive. That was one of the reasons I liked them so much.

Obed Ely, my math teacher/mentor, was a positive influence on me. I never saw him outside the classroom. We had absolutely no personal interaction that was in any way different from that which he had with all his students. He never knew the influence he had on me. I was not that different from anyone else. But suddenly, he was gone. All I knew was what I read in the papers: a statement made by the principal of the school, saying he didn't understand either. Back in those days, we didn't much talk about things like that. It just wasn't done in polite society.

All I could do was pour myself into my music. And I did.

Besides the musical opportunities available to me in New York, for the next seven years I had the blessing--and I use that word purposefully--of attending the National Music Camp at Interlochen, Michigan, each summer. That experience, without a doubt, did more to shape my life than anything. I often wonder what would have happened to me had I *not* been able to do that. I certainly would have been a very different person.

There I had the opportunity to make music with the likes of Howard Hanson, Frederick Fennel, Eugene Ormandy, Van Cliburn, and many friends who later grew up to be world-class musicians. We flew to Washington, D.C., and played at the White House for President Kennedy. We bussed down to Detroit to play for dignitaries at Cobo Hall, which was later renamed the Cobo Center. We paddled canoes down some of the great rivers of Michigan. Swam every day. Visited Mackinac Island and Sleeping Bear Sand Dunes. Played all sports and heard famous performers in every field of music play a concert every night. We recorded some great

Playing under Maestro Eugene Ormandy of the Philadelphia Orchestra (I'm in the trombone section, second row from the back, third in from the tuba player).

records for RCA. It was a fantastic experience, even though we simply took it all for granted.

But when you spend two months a year for seven years cut off from TVs, radios, and anything else that might connect you to the outside world, and instead play a full symphonic concert every week featuring the music of Brahms, Tchaikovsky, and other great composers, the "normal" world seems a long way off.

That was my real education. I cannot understand how local school boards these days can cavalierly decide to end the summer camp experience of kids by opening up before Labor Day, thus depriving their students of opportunities that are much more important than learning how to parse sentences or memorize important dates.

At Interlochen I learned to read. With no TV to clutter up my days, I walked around with a paperback book in my hip pocket. Since everyone else was doing it, too, we had literary discussions about books such as *Catcher in The Rye*, *1984*, *Animal Farm*, and *A Tale of Two Cities*.

By reading, I learned how to write. That's really how you learn things—by absorbing from the best and making it part of your everyday thinking. My English teacher once told me I would never become a writer because my spelling and handwriting were both atrocious. I wish she had lived to see me publish some twenty books. I didn't learn to write by having her teach me how to diagram sentences. That was a complete waste of time. To this day I know what a good phrase sounds like because I learned from the best writers of all time, not because I know what an incomplete sentence is. Whatever that means.

I learned to write by reading novels, while counting rests in the back of the orchestra, waiting for the part when the trombones got to play. I learned history by studying on my own, not by learning about Columbus sailing the ocean blue in 1492. I learned philosophy by reading philosophers, not by having someone teach me how Descartes knew he was alive because he was thinking about it.

It bothers me a great deal that I don't read as much as I used to. What's worse, I know why that is. The computer and television have shortened my attention span. It has become so obvious to me that I long ago stopped arguing with people who disagree. I've seen the change in my own life. I loved reading. I cannot imagine the effect technology is having on those modern members of the human race who grew up without the experience of reading a few

Winner of the Interlochen National Concerto Competition. Kresge Hall (1964). Orien Dalley, conductor.

Emory Brace Remington (1892–1971) was a trombonist and music teacher. His unique method made him one of the most well-known and influential trombone teachers in the world.

books a week as I did for more than 50 years.

Make no mistake. I couldn't write without my computer, and I would probably be bored and un-informed without my TV. But, oh, the price I paid for them both! I am as sure as one can be sure about any-thing that our species has paid much too high a price for that which we now consider indispensable. To be sure, we have gained the whole world, but I fear we have lost our souls in the process.

It took me eight years, from 1960 to 1968, before I realized that while I was learning how to make music, and while I was basking in the glow of creativity and artistic accomplishment, others my age were hav-ing quite a different experience and learning other things. I studied trombone with the late, great Emery Remington. He was the man who single-handedly transformed the art of trombone playing the world over. When foreign orchestras from Europe or even the So-viet Union came to Rochester to perform, their trombone section would immediately trundle off to the studio of the man we all called "The Chief" for a lesson or two.

When I came off the assembly line, I was a professional mu-sician. In the real world, however, things were different. In retro-spect, I should have seen it coming. In many ways, mine had been a sheltered life.

When water in a kettle gets hotter and hotter, eventually begin-ning to form steam that is bottled up with nowhere to go, it's only a matter of time before the lid pops off at its weakest point. The social kettle had begun to boil back in the 1950s.

The twentieth century witnessed an onslaught of epic proportions launched against the bastions of traditional society. Science seemed to erode the need for an outside force that created and sustains life, so religion started to decline. The "beat" generation began to haunt the by-ways of New York's Greenwich Village and beyond, inventing new ways to express a growing rage that they probably didn't even quite understand themselves. High-profile ministers and spiritual leaders were proven false, both in what they preached and in how they conducted their lives away from TV cameras. Politicians were tried and found wanting. Historians undermined national and international icons by "rewriting" history. They proved that what we learned about people ranging from Thomas Jefferson and Benjamin Franklin to Ike Eisenhower and Jack Kennedy may have been less than accurate. The Bible, long understood to be "the only infallible rule of faith and practice," ceased to be viewed by academics in the same way it used to be. "What did Jesus really say?" was replaced by "Was there really an historical Jesus?"

I was a professional musician — Eastman School of Music (1968)

This onslaught reached epic proportions when the surge of fundamentalist religion clashed with liberal spokesmen for science. The "faithful" seem to have gathered at opposite poles of right and left, conservative and liberal, believer and atheist, New Age and "old-time religion," there to hunker down behind ideological bunkers so as to hurl verbal bombs at the perceived enemy on the other side of the cultural divide.

What was left to believe in? Could we believe in anything? Was the answer to be found in "either/or"—*either* there is something true and real in which to place our faith *or* life is merely a cosmic accident to be survived?

What was left to believe in? The question was plastered all over the faces of sullen pop music icons who stared at the camera with blank expressions.

What was left to believe in? As usual, the artists among us saw it coming. Jackson Pollock and William de Kooning produced abstract art that ceased even trying to imitate normally perceived reality. Musicians as far removed as Igor Stravinsky and the Beatles resisted any attempt to be corralled within traditionally accepted forms.

What was left to believe in? Arthur Miller's *Death of a Salesman* and *A Streetcar Named Desire* made no attempt to make people feel good when they left the theater. Instead, art imitated life. Hollywood epitomized the breakdown of faith. Eventually, *Bonnie and Clyde, The Graduate, Easy Rider, Midnight Cowboy, The Last Picture Show, The Godfather*, and many more movies that followed scrapped the idea of "happily ever after."

What was left to believe in? Bumper stickers that proclaimed, "I'm spending my child's inheritance!" implied there wasn't going to be much of a future for younger generations. The earth seemed to be polluted beyond recovery. Wars and rumors of war filled the headlines. Vietnam was a living reality for thousands of young men while politicians at home saw it only as a partisan ploy to fire up their base. The body bags that brought so many tears to grieving parents were simply something to be exploited by others. After all, if we've already experienced, in television journalist Tom Brokaw's words, "the greatest generation," what's left for the rest of us? There was glory in coming home from a righteous war against institutionalized evil. But, as history has proved, Vietnam was a different beast.

By 1968 the lid blew off the kettle. Lyndon Johnson was forced to step down. Walter Cronkite himself traveled to Vietnam and saw what was happening, regardless of what the government propaganda machine was cranking out. Being the journalist that he was, he told us about it, and it wasn't pretty. President Johnson's own words best summed up the situation: "If I've lost Cronkite, I've lost the nation." He was right.

It didn't happen neatly within a span of ten years. It started early and continued later. But the '60s decade was as good a crash course in civil unrest as anyone might want.

As I write these words in 2022, it's still going on. Back then it was the overthrow of Jim Crow, white privilege, corrupt partisan politics, women's rights, the stratification of classes, inequality across the board, and a general attitude of "this is how you do it" authority. "My country, love it or leave it" was answered by a third alternative: "My country, change it."

By the summer of 2020, historians were beginning to compare the epidemic-ridden, environmental disaster, "Black Lives Matter," "Defund the Police" culture fraught with partisan political road-blocks and economic disparity to another time of history: the summer of 1968. Then, as now, there were riots in the streets, protest takeovers, troops firing on American citizens, opposing sides, and a feeling of hopelessness. This was followed by a worldwide pandemic, an epic failure of leadership, and economic collapse accompanied by unprecedented job losses and national despair.

Will the American experiment ever work? The problem is that it demands mature, compassionate, and empathetic citizens. I'm talking now about the experienced-based wisdom of Elders.

"What kind of government have you given us?" was the question posed to old Ben Franklin, after the Constitutional Convention finished his work.

"A republic," he answered, "if you can keep it."

His answer is not yet resolved.

That leads to the question that many of my generation faced as the tumultuous '60s began to wind down. By the time we finished our hitch in the army or college and were about to enter into adulthood, new possibilities unknown to our parents lay before us. We were forced to face the great unknown and new frontiers without a lot of guidance because many of our elders had marched in lockstep toward irrelevance, blinded by a misguided patriotism that was spawned in the fields of Europe and the seas of the South Pacific, but which fell apart in the sweltering heat of a Vietnam seen only on TV and a Korea that wasn't seen at all.

THE QUESTION

What path do you follow when suddenly faced with more choices than you can possibly understand?

Believe it or not, one of the great decisions I had to make in my life in 1968 was this: Do I shave my beard or quit teaching?

My answer was equally mystifying. I quit teaching. I haven't owned a razor of any kind since 1969.

It wasn't the beard. It was what the beard symbolized. I spent all ten years of the decade that ran from 1960 through 1970 and beyond in schools. Four years of high school, four years of college, and then three years of teaching in public schools and a session in seminary. For a brief time during the early '70s, I served as an assistant chaplain in a prison in Massachusetts. I am amazed when I look back at the two experiences and think about how much prisoners and school children share in common. Think about it:

- You have to be in attendance. It is against the law to not be there. You can't just leave if you want. If you try, they send the police after you.
- When a bell rings you get up and go wherever you're supposed to go and stay there until another bell rings.
- You eat what is put before you. Choices are extremely lim-

ited, and quite often the same food supplier delivers staples to both prisons and schools.

- You are not permitted to talk back to authority figures. If you do, you are punished.
- Once a day you are permitted out in the yard for exercise.
- There is a clearly perceived pecking order within the institution. Bullies are at the top and subservience is required. Otherwise, beatings might occur.
- At least in my day, uniforms were required. Certain clothing styles were not permitted and you were sent home if you broke the rules. (At least that part is different these days. But they have instituted metal detectors. We never had those. It's hardly a fair trade.)
- In order to progress sufficiently to get out, you had to prove you were "rehabilitated" by taking tests that showed you had learned enough to be a benefit to society.

I could probably go on, but that is enough to prove my point, however much tongue-in-cheek the whole list might have been. I think.

While all this was happening, there was another strictly observed code that was adhered to not only in school but even, in my social strata at least, throughout the rest of society as well. Beards were for beatniks and hippies. All other males were expected to be clean cut.

I hated shaving. I hated the time it took, the ritual, the primping, the staring in a mirror. When I got out of school and found myself in my first public school teaching job I said, "Finally!"

During the first summer vacation I let my beard grow. Then, when I had to go back to school in the fall, I was called into the principal's office and given a lecture. No beards. It was strict policy. I could shave or work. Period. And if I was fired from my job, the local draft board would snap me up and send me off to Vietnam. It was a clear choice.

I went home and shaved, but without fully realizing it I think I somehow knew my teaching days were over. Sometimes I am

A clean-shaven teacher. Lyons High School, New York (1969).

slow to realize, with my brain, what my heart has already decided. Looking back, I'm sure that on that drive home I decided I would never again put myself in a position in which I had to be under that kind of authority.

Jump ahead, for a moment, to the fall of 1971. I was now a student in seminary. Because my church background was Presbyterian, I took a course called Presbyterian Denominational Standards. It taught young clergy about the complexities of navigating the convoluted system of political control practiced by the Presbyterian Church.

At the end of the course, I realized I could never hack it. I would certainly rebel after a year or two. Then I discovered that different denominations had different systems of operating. New England Congregationalists, for instance, many of whom had recently joined together to form the relatively liberal United Church of Christ, believed in individual church autonomy. There was not a presbytery or system of bishops. Every church could decide issues for themselves. The ties that bound churches together were pretty loose, at least back then. These days, things have tightened up. But in the early days of the United Church of Christ, which was born during the fires of the '60s liberation marches and in the buses of Freedom Riders, it was the Wild West. No top-down control. And I soon learned that small churches, which paid equally small salaries, usually part-time, allowed an independent pastor like me a lot of individual freedom. If I offered what amounted to the equivalent of really good, full-time service, and kept folks happy and entertained, I'd have the advantage of setting my own schedule and doing things my way.

There was still control, of course. "Keeping folks happy" can sometimes be a full-time job. But it was the beginning of following my own instincts, at least as much as could be expected under existing conditions. I eventually came to regret the low pay. Sometimes I even felt taken advantage of when people expected full-time service for part-time pay. But on the whole, I learned to adjust.

I soon grew a beard, even though some in the congregation objected. I guess they thought a clean-shaven face was the best was to honor Jesus, who, in all the Sunday school pictures they showed to their kids, had a beard. But I never looked back.

During this decade there was another far more imposing organization looming over all of us. A moment ago, I mentioned that the draft board was waiting to snap up any and all loose souls who weren't lucky enough to have a deferment from military service. I can't possibly exaggerate what the Vietnam War did to everyone in this country. It towered over us like a colossus, and its menace governed absolutely everything else in American society. Young idealists today cannot comprehend what a shadowy, depressing, overwhelming power the draft board had over men of my generation.

As I look back through the lens of history, I am terribly torn. Countless thousands of Vietnam vets went off to fight because they felt it was their duty to serve their country. They remembered the patriotic pride of World War II, a needed war if ever there was one. The Korean conflict hadn't yet really sunk in. Media was not as ever-present then as it is now. It was possible to go for days without hearing about what was happening, and many of the folks who came home didn't want to talk about their experience. Besides, according to the newspapers, Korea wasn't a "war." It was a "police action."

But Vietnam was different.

Listening to those who full-out lied to the American people, the John Kennedys, the Lyndon Johnsons, the Bob McNamaras, the Richard Nixons, and many others, we now know how much politics was involved, and how many young men died so that politicians back home could get re-elected. Nowadays, that's an established fact. But this was the '60s. We hadn't learned that yet.

A lot of young people had caught on, however. The protests were loud and violent. Vietnam ignited a war between liberal and conservative. The odd thing was that, in the wildly successful TV show, *All in the Family*, when Archie Bunker sat in his chair arguing with "Meathead," his son-in-law, a lot of people didn't get it. They sided with Archie.

When the debacle finally ended in abject failure, many of the troops who came home were treated with contempt. The unadulterated hatred that had flourished during a decade of war, and the ignominious retreat that marked its conclusion, had uncovered too many raw nerve endings.

I think that may finally be changing. There seems to be a greater respect, now that people's ideas have had a chance to solidify and become more clearly stated. But it took a long time, and many Vietnam vets died without knowing they would one day be seen as heroes. All in all, it was a tragic time, and like most historical epochs, there were no final solutions to make things right. Unfortunately, as is so often the case, many don't live "happily ever after."

At the time this was all going down, however, I missed a lot of it. I don't say that proudly at all. As I said earlier, I spent a good part of the decade in a practice room. The riots in many cities didn't really register in my brain until I went back to school in Rochester, New York, as the summer of 1967 ended and I saw burnt-out buildings and experienced the aftermath of what must have been terrible to behold. This was the world I would have to enter in one, short, year. When they drew the lottery numbers for the draft, my number was 33. It was a virtual certainty that if I didn't do something, I was going off to Vietnam.

When I went to my draft board to register, spending the day in my underwear, getting poked and prodded, and taking reams of tests, I didn't know any better. I told the truth.

They asked me if I was comfortable alone in the woods at night. Of course, I was! I hunted and fished alone for days on end.

They asked me if I had ever shot a rifle. Of course, I had! I had been a crack shot ever since I was a kid back in 1957. By now I was a regular Davy Crockett.

Well, kind of …

They asked if I had ever done any backpacking. Need I say more?

Halfway through, it finally occurred to me that I might be signing my death warrant. I might as well have written "grunt" on my forehead. I was perfect infantry material. Young, strong, in shape, able to walk or run for miles, emotionally pliable, and a good shot to boot. What was I thinking?

A crack shot since 1957 – Jimmy Willis, 11 years old.

Davy Crockett? —
Palmyra, NY (1967)

Obviously, I needed a plan. When I graduated in the spring of 1968, I still didn't have one.

There is an innocence about being a 22-year-old optimist. You always figure something will work out.

And it did. I had heard through the musician's grapevine that there might be an opening for a trombone player in the 5th Army Band stationed near Chicago. I got in touch with them and arranged for an audition. My parents lived outside of Chicago at the time. They had recently returned from a stint in Australia, where the American Oil Company had sent my father to refurbish operations. They were now living and working out of the Chicago office.

(I have to insert an interlude here. Dad was the top AMOCO dog in Australia while he was over there. When he and mom decided to take a short vacation away from duties, they booked a cruise to Tasmania. While on the cruise, the captain learned he had a big shot on board, and mom and dad were asked to eat at the captain's table. My father often told the story with great delight. But one night, when some guests were visiting the house, Dad again recounted the experience, ending, in an offhanded manner, "Of course, we were asked to dine at the captain's table." One of the guests, who obviously had learned how to push Dad's buttons, said, "Do you mean you paid all that money and had to eat with the crew?" I'll never forget it!)

At any rate, my plan was to head out to Chicago, stay with my parents for a few days, take the audition, get accepted, of course, and spend the next three years of my life in the army. Just in case, on the way out of town, I stopped off at Lyons, New York, to put in a token meeting to apply for the job of instrumental music teacher at the local high school. It looked like a good gig. There would be three people in the music department: one doing the string and orchestra program, one doing the band and brass program, and one doing the vocal program. I was heading for a stint in the army. I really didn't take it seriously. I was a professional musician, not a music teacher. It had been a hard and fast doctrine at Eastman: "Those who can, do. Those who can't, teach!"

With no real sense of urgency, I drove to Chicago, had a great reunion with my parents, and then drove out to Fort Sheridan to meet with the guy who conducted the band.

He loved my audition, especially when he discovered I played jazz. Turned out he had a jazz sextet that played gigs in Chicago when the army band wasn't touring. He wanted me to play in his group, collect union scale for gigs with his combo, and anchor the trombone section in the post band. Of course, he didn't have an opening for trombone in the band at the moment, but he would call me a harp player until one turned up. It was my first exposure to the way the army did things. After a year or so, when it would come time for a transfer, he would recommend me wherever I wanted to go.

"Hawaii?"

"Sure! No problem!"

He would even recommend that I skip the compulsory six-month training school that followed boot camp, telling the army I was too advanced for that, being from Eastman and all.

I went back to my folk's house and told them that my future was secure.

Then disaster struck. I received notice that I had failed the army physical. Something about too many white blood cells coursing through my body. It may have had something to do with the fact that I was recovering from a recent case of mononucleosis. It could have been attributed to the fact that I was so nervous before my physical that I had spent the night partying with an old friend, who actually had to drive me to my physical the next morning because I was too wasted to drive myself.

Whatever the case, they told me not to die on government property and please check in with them again in six months.

I couldn't wait six months. I needed a job. Then, one evening, while sitting with my mom and dad, never realizing how nervous and stressed they were, I got a call out of the blue from the high school I had stopped at on my way out of town in New York. After much consideration, they wanted to offer me the job. Would I be interested in becoming their band teacher? And could I start in two weeks because they ran a summer music program? And, by the way, when six months rolled around, I would have a draft deferment because I would be a public-school music teacher.

So, the army lost a recruit, the Chicago jazz scene lost a budding star, the world of classical music lost a symphony trombonist, and I became a public-school music teacher. I didn't even think about it much, but the course of my life was forever changed.

It sounds strange to me now, but I was never really worried.

Public school teacher —
Lyons, NY (1969)

The innocence of youth assumed something good would happen. Now I wonder. Was that very innocence a trust that somehow the Cosmos would turn out the way it was supposed to turn out? Was my naiveté in fact a neophyte's acceptance of fate, or, as I would soon come to call it, an act of God?

Sometimes I long for those days when simple trust ruled my life. Nowadays, when I have to work for such acceptance and consider it a virtue, I can't often find it. I want to relax and trust that things will happen as they should, but it is very difficult. Isn't it strange that back when I had no real faith in anything, I accepted my destiny without a thought? But now, after having learned so much about the operations of Spirit, I fret and squirm under life's vicissitudes.

And so it happened that as the '60s came to an end I found myself finally free from worry about being drafted, about having a job, a purpose, and I was finally able to get married and begin life, which I soon did. The boy who began the decade hating school was now a school teacher, who would soon learn why he hated school so much. Life is strange, full of twists and turns. Sometimes, all you can do is hold on and hope to survive.

Cosmo and Me

Chapter 3:

The Great Illusion (the 1970s)

THE CULTURE

Can anyone ever be the same after experiencing Vietnam and Watergate? To say nothing of the Muppets, who seemed to symbolize the era. They were pretend caricatures who echoed reality and, in the process, became more real than life itself. They even became the teachers of our kids. If life is a stage, all mirrors and illusion, and if the possibility exists that we all might be puppets on a string, maybe there's only one thing to do: Become a minister and begin your search for the Holy Grail.

I wonder sometimes if, like other animal species, we have the ability to sense when conditions around us are about to change. We may not be able to explain the feeling. Maybe we don't even recognize it as such. But something deep within tells us that the weather vane is moving ahead of a storm front, either physical or psychological, and we react in ways that seem totally out of character. We tense up somehow. We overreact. We feel an overwhelming oppression of some kind. Our minds can't describe it, but our body registers the effect. It knows.

How else do I explain my actions early in 1970? I was finished with college. I had a teaching job and some really neat students. The draft board was no longer the bane of my existence. I was married to a woman I loved and who loved me in return. My income wasn't great, but it was adequate ... barely. I was able to supplement it with music gigs of various kinds. I was playing at dances, conducting church choirs, and performing with the Syracuse Symphony, a job I fell into when their first trombonist was involved in a car crash and they needed a substitute who could come in with no rehearsal. These all contributed to paying the rent. I was able to hunt and fish a great deal. On the surface, things were going well.

So why did I find myself sitting on the couch one day, pistol in hand, contemplating suicide?

I think my body recognized that there was a storm coming and was warning me. I sensed in my soul that which my brain didn't yet comprehend, and I was afraid. Perhaps my two mentors, who had also been down this road and had both committed suicide, felt the coming change way before I was old enough to understand it myself.

The 1960s, I now believe, can best be described as a bridge decade. American culture changed. It took a long time, in human terms. Even though there had been unrest in the streets and violent reactions in many places in society, we gradually got used to them. The temperature was rising, but so slowly that we had time to acclimate ourselves and thus didn't realize what was happening. But something was dying during those years, make no mistake about it—something that consisted of not only a way of life, but, even more important, the way we *thought* about our way of life. For good or ill, we were all confronting the death of who we were, as individuals, and as part of American culture.

That was probably a good thing. There was a lot of negative activity that needed to be dealt with beneath the surface during those days. Racism, sexism, ageism, political corruption, bigotry— those were all evils that needed to be brought to the surface and dealt with. They needed to die. But death is never easy, no matter in what form we experience it.

Each time we are confronted with the end of an era, a forced, unexpected change in our cultural ambiance, our emotions are hotwired to experience it as death, an ending of what was. We must process stages that Elizabeth Kubler-Ross, in her wonderful 1969 book titled *On Death and Dying*, identified as denial, bargaining, anger, and depression, until we can finally arrive at acceptance and can then begin anew. That's what became obvious by 1970.

Our first experience of such a cultural death was denial. "Don't make so much of it! It's just a passing fad. The good old days will come back soon. Just wait and ignore it. It's all happened before."

But when social upheaval could no longer be put off, the next step was bargaining. "If, somehow, we can just hang on and get through this, we'll never commit those sins of hubris again.... We'll change if things just settle down.... If we can elect a guy from a different political party, things will return to normal."

Those are all if/then statements. It amounts to bargaining.

But anger soon follows. We get mad at any strawman we can erect to take the blame for whatever is happening that upsets our comfortable lifestyle. We place onto a group—or even an individual—the blame for what's happening. "It's the Democrat's fault.... It's the Republican's fault.... It's our parent's fault.... It all started when they took prayer out of the schools.... It's the blacks! It's the whites! It's the feminists! It's the poor! It's the rich!"

Find a group, remind others that things were better before *they* took over, instigate an angry response, and things will return to the way they used to be. That's a classic anger-type response.

When we experience anger, however, it almost always eventually turns into depression. Our civilization is not very well adjusted, at least in terms of Darwinian evolution and the principle of the survival of the fittest. Those who are out there on the front lines have an outlet for their anger, however misguided it is. The rest of us usually internalize things. We punish ourselves rather than others. We are not among the fittest who survive by, even appropriately, directing our anger outward. We turn on the TV news to deliberately make us feel worse. We *want* to hear about the latest tragedy. We *revel* in feeding our depression. Call it a psychological flaw—and it probably is—but unless we are totally innocent, which rarely happens, we can never be angry for long without getting depressed. Then, once depressed, we constantly encourage it. It's not that we really *want* to feel depressed. We don't. But once it begins, depression takes on a life of its own. In demonic fashion, it can possess us so thoroughly that we might even find ourselves sitting on a couch with a pistol in our hand.

I have found, however, through both personal and professional experience, that depression is a necessary, unpleasant stage that we must endure if we are ever to come out on the other side and begin a new phase of life. This applies to both cultures and individuals.

Please understand that I'm talking about run-of-the-mill, garden-variety depression brought on by cultural upheaval. Full-blown chemical depression, which feels the same but lasts forever if not treated, is quite a different beast.

That said, depression can be experienced in two ways.

The first and most common feeling of depression is the down-in-the-dumps, woe-is-me type, where we feel sorry for ourselves, get cranky, yell at the dog, go to bed, medicate ourselves with drink, drugs, or ice cream, and just wait it out.

That is certainly not pleasant, but we all experience it. We even talk and sing about the "blues," and the country music industry would soon go broke if we suddenly found a cure. Unless we get stuck, which can happen and is nothing to joke about, the cure is usually time and space to ourselves. Remember that: "time and space to ourselves." It's about to become very important.

But there is another valuable, constructive way to experience depression. Understanding that depression is a normal and appropriate part of the process that must follow the death of one stage and the beginning of another, it can be embraced, serving as an analytical tool for examining and envisioning a future different from the one to which we thought we were headed. This is hard enough for an individual to pull off. For an entire culture, it's darn near impossible. Cultures have too many moving parts. You just can't get enough people to respond appropriately at the same time, so the death of a cultural ideology is almost always followed by social upheaval and catastrophe. The social pendulum swings from one extreme to its opposite.

Individuals experience such things individually. *I* may not be able to make an entire culture respond, but I can do something about *myself*—a person within that culture.

In the case of an individual, then, depression is a red light that will be followed by green as soon as we are ready to go on. But what do we do in the meantime while we're waiting for the light to change?

A few paragraphs ago I mentioned that the supposed sickness of depression needs the medicine of "time and personal space." But think about that carefully. Time and personal space are exactly the ingredients we need for personal introspection and self-evaluation. It *can't* be an accident! Depression *must* be telling us that its function is to lead us to another future, a new insight, a new beginning. Denial, bargaining, anger, and depression have been called the stages of grief—of death and dying. Maybe they should be called, instead, the stages of hope—of life and living. It *cannot* be a coincidence that the final stage is acceptance, the acceptance of a new future not yet understood.

"A new future not yet understood." That's the key, isn't it? But whatever kind of future *can* there be except one that is not yet understood? We can argue forever about the nature of time, whether it is circular, linear, or something else. But the fact remains that most of us experience it, most of the time, as past, present, and future. The future can be frightening just because it *is* unknown.

That's why we do our best to insulate ourselves with insurance policies and retirement accounts. The story of the person who saves for a rainy day and then unexpectedly gets hit by a truck is reported with tragic irony and feels chilling because such a circumstance is often either our secret fear or a supposed justification for our own failure to prepare properly.

So depression, when it is induced by a fear of what tomorrow may bring, can be just the tool we need to conquer our apprehensions and step into a new life stage of maturity with acceptance of our own mortality and fragility.

Acceptance of a future not yet understood is called, by religious folks, faith. The writer of the biblical book of Hebrews called it the "assurance of things hoped for, the conviction of things not seen." It's what allows us to get up in the morning, having at least some trust that today, although still an unknown quantity, will be worth living. Without some kind of faith, we all would probably perish. Sad to say, some people do. After all, out there at the edge of faith lies the boundary of despair. Many folks, such as my two mentors who crossed that boundary, die, sometimes by their own hands, without hope.

But faith, like every other living thing, can be fed and exercised, making it grow stronger, pushing the boundary farther out ahead.

These thoughts never entered my head as I sat on my couch, contemplating ending my life for reasons I didn't understand. But now that I look back at that moment, it is obvious that I faced a crossroads. Would I live or die?

Thankfully, I got past that moment and chose life. But I don't think the decision was mine alone. You see, that moment prepared me for what was to come. I soon experienced a religious conversion. I experienced God. A year later, I entered seminary.

In retrospect, God has a sense of humor. I see that now. I didn't see it then, but I see it now.

I had a good, steady, music gig going by then. Thursday, Friday, and Saturday nights found me playing with one of the hottest retro bands in town. Believe it or not, it was a banjo band. But it was electrified, and it rocked with four recent Eastman grads, a rhythm banjo to hold us together, and an old guy who knew every sing-a-long song ever written. It sounds funny now. Banjo bands have declined in popularity these days, but back then we were the featured house band for a place that seated about 400 people and packed in twice that number on Saturday nights. They came to eat pizza, drink beer, and sing songs that were at least 40 years old, along with the banjo version of pop tunes of the era such as "Aquarius" and "Sunny." We even threw in our own version of orchestral favorites such as the overture from *William Tell* (you might know it as the theme from the *Lone Ranger* TV show) and a wild rendition of Brahms' *Hungarian Rhapsody*. We rocked the place every night.

I got the job pretty much by accident. I had played with a Dixieland band twice a week at an amusement park during the summer before we started up. I guess I must have established a reputation because when the owner of the Golden Nugget in Rochester, New York, wanted to build a restaurant/bar around a band, the lead banjo guy, Drew Freck, thought of me. Drew has gone on to become a national banjo champion, establishing quite a reputation. He is a well-known phenom. But back then, we were all just starting out. We were already hot enough, however, to play for some big-time political conventions when they came to town. We hobnobbed with Nelson Rockefeller and James Buckley, for instance, who were big in national politics. We traveled quite a bit and got to experience a lot of different kinds of venues.

Almost every Saturday night a particular husband and wife could be counted on to come early and set up right by the bandstand. They always brought their little daughter. They had enough money to go out drinking and carousing, but not enough to pay for a babysitter. We felt sorry for the little girl. It was always loud and raucous, especially near the bandstand, and was really no place for a kid her age. So we invited her up on the bandstand every night, built a corral of sorts with our instrumental cases, made a bed for her out of our coats, and let her fall asleep in the midst of all the din. Ah, the sweet innocence and adaptability of youth!

One night she didn't show up. When we asked her parents why, they said she had the mumps.

Oh, oh! A week later half the band was out sick. Let me assure you that when a young, 22-year-old trombone player gets the mumps—and not just in his throat—it is a serious condition. All I could do was stay home and stay in bed. Two weeks' worth of bed rest. "And don't move!" the doctor said.

I was forced to stay home, watch what TV there was back in those days of three black-and-white channels, read, and listen to the radio.

It was the radio that changed my life. One day I found myself listening to a radio evangelist, and he made me angry. I don't remember what he said, but it must have been pretty potent because I asked my wife to get my Bible off the shelf, the one that they had given me back in Detroit when I joined the church and told my confirmation class that "I---I---I w-w-w-want t-t-t-to be a p-p-p-preacher."

It was in pristine condition, still in the box that had never been opened. I looked up the passage that the radio evangelist was quoting and began to read just to prove him wrong.

And then something happened. To this day I can't really describe it, but I remember that moment with vivid clarity. One minute I was a cynical, smart-alecky skeptic who had long since outgrown any childhood spiritual inclinations he might have once had. The next I was believer. It was a classic conversion experience.

That day I did the most courageous thing I've ever done in my life. I asked my wife to pray with me. We were close and shared everything, but this was taking trust to a whole new level. We were together, she kneeling by the couch and me still flat on my back. And I said the first real prayer that I have ever prayed out loud. The sense of forgiveness, and acceptance, and peace, was palpable to us both.

Say what you will, you who have never experienced an overwhelming conversion experience. I don't doubt your doubt. I even forgive your snide remarks and Freudian explanations. But unless you've had a similar experience, don't question mine. These days, I may look back with greater understanding and more intellectual metaphors. I may realize in greater detail the psychological reasons that lie behind such a commitment. I may even wonder if what we experienced that day was simply an emotional reaction to pain and worry. But I will never forget the complete and utter transformation that occurred.

Unless it has happened to you, I won't argue with you about it. But before that prayer I felt blind. After, I could see. No one will ever take it away from me. From doubter to transformed believer.

I might understand it in a completely different way these days, but back then it was powerful and, quite literally, changed my life.

That's why I say God has a sense of humor. What else but some kind of divine intelligence could have reached out to a religious kid who had lost his religion, let him mellow through a years-long, world-class depression, fostered his spirituality by bringing him into close contact with the death of mentors, and then had the old Bible from the early years on the shelf at just the right time, ready at hand to be triggered by a little girl with the mumps? Halfway through my reading of the Gospel of John, I became a real Christian in heart as well as tradition, and I never looked back.

Well, maybe I looked back a little, but we'll get to that. Meanwhile, however, within a very short time I had quit my job, sold my house, left a career in music and teaching, horrified everyone I knew except our drummer, who was already a devout Christian, and signed up for a seminary that was 500 miles away.

THE QUESTION

Is there really something More, something Other?
Or is it just an empty promise accessible only by "faith?"

When I walked through the doors of Gordon Conwell Theological School, which had once boasted none other than the late, great Billy Graham on its board of directors, but who in my time had been replaced by his son Franklin, I hadn't even read the Bible. I knew the New Testament fairly well, at least from a layman's point of view, and was somewhat familiar with many stories from the Old Testament, but that was about it. It never occurred to me that I was in way over my head. My passion was greater than my performance.

I lasted for only a year and a half.

In the early 1970s, many conservative Christian people my age thought the world was about to come to an end. Hal Lindsey had just written his book *The Late Great Planet Earth*, which is based on

GORDON-CONWELL THEOLOGICAL SEMINARY										
SO. HAMILTON, MASSACHUSETTS 01982										

Eastman School of Music of

NAME ___ WILLIS, JAMES MURRAY ___

ADDRESS ___ 27 East Williamson Rd. ___

Marion, New York 14505

MATRICULATED ___ September, 1971 ___

UNDERGRADUATE SCHOOL AND DEGREE Univ. of Rochester

ADVANCED STANDING ___

GRADUATED ___ WITH DEGREE OF ___

WITHDREW ___

YEAR	CAT.NO.	TITLE OF COURSE	GRD.	CREDIT	GRD. PTS.	YEAR	CAT.NO.	TITLE OF COURSE	GRD.	CREDIT
Fall, 1971	CH 101	Church to Reformation	B	1	3					
	GL 101	Basic Greek I	B+	1	3					
	MC 101	Intro. to Theol. Ed.	P	1	-					
	NT 101	New Testament Survey	C	1	2					
	MC 201	Denom. Stds. - Presby.	B	1	3					
		Field Education	1 Unit							
Winter, 1972	CH 102	Modern Christianity	B	1	3					
	GL 102	Basic Greek II	B	1	3					
	PC 101	Man and His Relation.	P	1	-					
	OT 199	Old Testament Survey	C+	1	2					
	MC 201	Denom. Stds.- Cong.	C	1	2					
Fall, 1972	ME 241	Chris. Appr. to Non-Chris. Religions	B-	1	3					

KEY TO GRADING SYSTEM: A-OUTSTANDING: B-GOOD; C-SATISFACTORY; D-PO BUT PASSING; E-CONDITIONAL FAILURE; F-FAILURE; WP-WITHDREW PASSING; WITHDREW FAILING. GRADE POINTS ARE AWARDED ON FOLLOWING BASIS: A-4; C-3; D-1; E-0; F-0. FOR THE PURPOSE OF TRANSFER, A COURSE CREDIT IS EQUIVAL TO 1 SEMESTER HOURS. STUDENT IS ENTITLED TO HONORABLE DISMISSAL UNL OTHERWISE INDICATED.

DATE *August 28 1974* Ones) *L.S. Herman*

It never occurred to me that I was in way over my head (September 1971).

his interpretation of biblical prophecy. When it was released by the Zondervan Publishing Company in 1970, it shot to the top of the *New York Times* bestseller nonfiction list and stayed there for the next ten years. No one can dispute the "best-selling" label. The book was a huge commercial success. As for the "nonfiction" part, well, that remains to be seen.

In 1976 the book was made into a movie narrated by Orson Welles. To this day you'll find *LGPE*, as it came to be known, in the library of just about every evangelical minister in America. In 1984 Lindsey followed it up with his interpretation of The Revelation of St. John, which is the final book of the Bible. He called this one *There's a New World Coming*. Sales for that book were off the charts as well.

But in 1971 and '72 I was a struggling seminary student, busily trying to learn Greek, church history, systematic theology, and denominational standards. There were five women in the entire school. All the rest were men, mostly young white guys like me. I had the idea that someday I might become the pastor of a small church out in the boonies somewhere, where I would hunt and fish to my heart's delight, raise vegetables, utilize my survival skills to survive the coming collapse, rest assured in my ministerial draft deferment, and let the world take care of itself!

New translations of the Bible were coming out back then, seemingly every day. The faithful old King James Version was turning into a dinosaur, except in the South, of course. The fundamentalist folks down there weren't about to give up their Schofield Bibles. Many of them still haven't, for that matter. But what did I know back then?

For that matter, what did any of us know? We had no idea that basic social precepts were in flux. We still thought the world was waiting to welcome us with open arms. That was the success story we were taught. "Build a better mousetrap, and the world will beat a path to your door." I just assumed I would enter the world of religion, survive whatever was going to happen in the future, obtain some modest fame, and make enough money to get by.

I know, it sounds crazy. How could a person expect to live happily ever after and also accept that there was "a new world coming" after the collapse of civilization that would take place just before the return of Jesus Christ?

That kind of intellectual dichotomy might be explained by all the other changes of cultural evolution that were taking place at the same time. Vietnam had rocked the nation, but the Nixon scandal was looming larger every year, and others my age were supposedly returning from their trip into sex, drugs, and rock & roll. If the truth were known, most of us, at least the friends I knew in church circles, missed out on all that. If we knew the words to a few Beatles songs we thought we were cool. That was enough, so we just struggled on.

When I say I "struggled," I'm referring to more than my studies. Academically, I was floundering and beginning to suspect it. But the biggest problem was money. My fondest memory of those times was one dreadful Friday night when I added up our bills and discovered that we owed $298 by Monday—no ifs, ands, or buts. I looked over at my wife, who was calmly reading a magazine on the couch, and said, "We're in trouble. We'd better pray."

She looked back at me, the aspiring clergyman who was going to win the world for Christ by teaching people to have faith, smiled a beatific smile, and said, "Has it come to that?"

We laughed about it for a long time.

This story has a postscript. We did pray about it, of course, and the very next day we got a check in the mail for $300. A church that had somewhat supported me in the past had some money left over in their mission budget and decided to send it to us.

Now, what church ever has money "left over" in its mission budget? But they did, so we paid our bills and wound up with $2 extra. Know what we did? We went out and bought a cheap bottle of wine to celebrate! Who says God doesn't have a sense of humor?

Those were tough days, for sure. One night my jaw was hurting, and I didn't know why. The more I thought about it, the more I realized that it had been months since I had eaten any meat that I had to chew. It was too expensive. I never told my wife about it, but I gnawed on an old running shoe after she went to bed, just for the exercise. That kind of thing stays with you through life.

In some ways, those were simple days. The professor was still lord of his classroom, and students were supposed to mentally genuflect whenever the teachers issued their edicts. Most of what we were taught was based on "expert" opinions previously formed during the laborious academic days of the '50s.

The process was straightforward. Professors, who had written the textbooks we used, pontificated. We believed it, wrote it down in our workbooks, and were then tested to make sure we walked the proper academic line. At our ordinations we were further grilled and, if we passed muster by our betters, were promoted to full-fledged novice "experts" ourselves. Those who went on to earn advanced degrees still had to pay their dues, but if they did, they were rewarded by becoming the new generation of installed and revered "experts" who were quoted in all the magazines. Their work was then taught to the next generation. It was a self-perpetuating system.

In order to earn a doctorate, you had to publish new research in a subject that had never before been written about. As you might expect, that narrowed the field a good bit with each passing year. How do you find new things to write about when the Christian Church has been studying and publishing material ever since the Apostle Paul first got arrested? Most of the good stuff was long since taken. As a result, papers were defended that had titles such as "Augustine's Use of the Oxford Comma" and "Martin Luther's Third Treatise and the Birth of Existentialism."

That's an exaggeration, of course, but you get the idea. We used to say that more and more was being learned about less and less, and if the trend continued we would soon arrive at the point where absolutely everything was known about nothing.

Such an attitude promotes skepticism. In my case, I decided to spend the rest of my life in small-town churches, far from the academic world. Life in the university had lost its glamour. Instead, I planned on helping a few people get through the vicissitudes of daily living. It was more practical. Now, from the viewpoint of half a century later, I got it about halfway right.

I have to admit it, though: Part of me died in seminary or at least went to sleep. The thrill of mystery and magic was gone. From then on, everything seemed to be a bit hum-drum, if you know what I mean. There may have been "giants" in the old days, "heroes of old, men of renown," but in my time, the "giants" who were supposed to be satisfying my thirst for spiritual growth had let me down big time. Things were never quite the same after that.

In the back of my mind, I never stopped looking and hoping. I became a pastor, was ordained even without graduating, and achieved a modicum of success. Such things were easier back in those days. After I spent a year in my first church, I dropped out of seminary "just for a little while so I could help get my new church off the ground."

I finally earned my master's degree 20 years later. Meanwhile, I went on to study on my own, and I learned a lot—much more than I would have in a formal school setting. I studied not only what interested me, but what I needed to know. Not very many of my parishioners cared very much about whether Daniel wrote the whole biblical book that carried his name or whether he wrote in Aramaic or Greek. They had more immediate concerns. My professors, however, had seemed to think that such things were important to the Christian laity.

It took 40 years to answer the deep, abiding questions that rose up every once in a while, whenever I slowed down enough to think about them, because life continued at what, looking back from my present perspective of relative comfort, now seems to be a frantic pace. Recently, I've developed the opinion that life throws too much at people during the decade of their twenties:

- They have to make the leap from dependent child to independent, hopefully well-adjusted adult.
- They have to learn how to do everything from balancing a checkbook to maintaining an automobile, while learning how to shop and cook.
- They have to take on the full responsibilities and duties of a new career.
- They usually get married. At least, back then they did. Living together was simply not an option unless you were from some exotic location such as California.
- Sometimes they even buy a house and have to learn how to fix things when they inevitably break down.
- They often have children and need to learn parenting skills.
- They suddenly have civic duties.

It's too much. Each one of those responsibilities is a chore in and of itself. Together, they form a recipe for disaster. It's no wonder I almost opted out at the beginning.

Take just one of the above categories—that of raising children. Two years after I left seminary, I found myself, I don't know how (well, I guess I must have known how, but barely!), a father of two kids.

Much to my surprise, I soon discovered that things had changed. Parents in the '70s were expected to be totally different from parents in the '50s. I had no template to follow.

Take, for instance, the art of keeping the kids occupied while you tried to help fix dinner. In my youth, children entertained themselves and kept clear until they were called to dinner, whereupon they complained and tried to squeeze out a few more minutes for whatever they were doing. But when *my* kids were young, we had a new educational tool called the television. That changed everything. Enter Jim Henson and his Muppets.

Old Boomers have a deep, dark secret. Whenever those of us who were born between 1946 and about 1955 gather to toss back a few beverages, whine about the old days, and declare that everything has changed for the worse, our secret eventually comes out. Boomers are sheepish about it because it's not politically correct to say it, but we can't get around it. "Avoidance" isn't a word that's found in Boomer vocabulary, anyway. We are, after all, the confrontational tribe who like to think that we helped bring about civil rights and an end to the war in Vietnam. And maybe we did.

Anyway, the secret is, to wit: When we, as youngsters, gathered with our families in front of the Motorola to watch the *Ed Sullivan Show* on Sunday evenings, we secretly thought Ed's European puppet mania was a bit weird, even though the whole riff was aimed right at what he called "youngsters." In other words, us.

Topo Gigio? Too sappy. The Man in the Box? Senior Winces was a very strange old man. The Marionettes from Outer Czechoslovakia? Give me a break! (Jim Henson obviously had a different take on all this, but Boomers didn't know him yet.)

Afternoon TV wasn't much better. Kookla, Fran, and Ollie whined too much, and Lamb Chop was immature. Besides, parents liked them. Speaking of parents, Boomer parents laughed out loud at Charley McCarthy, but Boomer kids never quite saw the point. We watched, though, because there was nothing else on after school except Spanky and the gang, which is a whole 'nother story. Puppet shows may have had Mom's seal of approval, but as soon as Sheri Lewis signed off, Flash Gordon and Ming the Merciless came on. No doubt about it, even back then, we were looking for technological flash. We just didn't know it yet.

Howdy Doody was a little better, but something about that disjointed, prancing, bent-forward walk was upsetting. Besides, no one could take seriously anything said by a puppet Indian maiden named "Princess Summer-Fall-Winter-Spring." Clarabelle the Clown wasn't much of an improvement, even if he did eventually grow up to read the weather on the *Today* show. How could you trust someone whose shtick was to spray seltzer water on people while never saying anything? It was surreal. And the peanut gallery! Who were those kids?

Soupy Sales did some neat stuff with puppets. But the only time you could watch him was when you were home sick from school because he came on at lunchtime. Captain Kangaroo's Mister Moose was funny. But really, puppets were simply something to be tolerated. They were not nearly as cool as Davy Crockett and Zorro.

It wasn't until we Boomers had kids of our own that we finally found puppets we could embrace to our collective bosom. Kermit and company—called Muppets rather than puppets—invaded our lives and found a home, especially because they came on right before dinner.

Sesame Street changed everything. The show was definitely not for kids. Or if it was, at least it had adult levels that could really be appreciated. "C is for cookie...." Now, that had style. And Oscar the Grouch! He looked just like your boss. Grover, telling you the difference between "near" and "far"? It was worth putting up with Mr. Rogers' puppets just to be on the right PBS channel when the kids told you "How to get to Sesame Street."

Ethnic Muppets were what the new America was all about. Although the show had moderate success in foreign countries, there was no doubt about where the action took place. It was the Big Apple all the way and hard to transport.

(In 1997, a joint team of Israeli and Palestinian TV producers tried to spin off a local version in which Sesame Street existed in a happy neighborhood filled with Jewish and Arab kids. It never got off the ground. Daoud Kuttab, a Palestinian media executive, explained the situation to *Voice of America* in March 1997: "To be believable and authentic, and to be credible to children, it couldn't be too far away from reality." Since then, I understand, they managed to work out the kinks and air a very successful version, but back then, highly decorated green and orange talking socks with bulbous eyes weren't the problem. Kids could handle that. It was just that their TV Sesame Street had no check points, armed guards, and barbed wire. They couldn't relate.)

When the Muppets got their own prime time show the gloves came off. No need to please the Board of Education now. Skip the kid stuff. This was adult-funny! Piggy and Kermit came out of the closet ready to bring it on! (Hi-Yah!!!) Zoot, the Charlie Parker wannabe, was the guy who used to play sax in my garage band. ("How do you get to Carnegie Hall? Practice!") "Pigs in Space" even dared poke fun at Trekkies. This was good stuff!

There was more to come. It seemed that the end was nowhere in sight. The Muppets moved to the big screen. Success at last! Henson had told Boomers that we were supposed to like puppets, and because Jim was cool, we tried. But now we could really dig it. This was finally for *us*. Three movies, great music, good stories, and terrific reviews.

Then it happened. The ultimate trip! Yoda got his own gig. Imagine it. A Zen-master Muppet who taught people how to imagine a new universe while fighting with swords. Okay—lightsabers. Whatever. It was the same thing. After nine hundred years Yoda still hadn't learned to speak English very well, but he knew everything else. He was puppet-warm and fuzzy but also wise and strong, holding his own even against that classically trained artistic icon Sir Alec Guinness. Yoda was the puppet that people had been searching for ever since an upright humanoid creature with an opposing thumb figured out that he could talk to his own hand and make people believe. Yoda was the culmination of puppet evolution. State of the art. Now he had his own movie. He even opened the door for Ewoks—big puppets with whole people inside of them!

But what did Hollywood do as soon as technology gave them a chance? They digitized Yoda! He became a cartoon character made up of 1s and 0s. What's up with that? You can't improve on a puppet with a warm hand up his..... Well, it just wasn't natural. Sure, he could now bounce around the room with a light saber and do gymnastics better than Mary Lou Retton, but it just wasn't the same.

Remember now that some Boomers who complained hadn't worn anything except one-hundred-percent cotton and virgin wool since the summer of 1968. They had saved whales and hugged trees. A few of them patrolled for turtles and counted their condors before they were hatched. To them, computer-driven actors were just high-tech cartoons. That's what made 2008 such a disaster when George Lucas went even further. He made a cartoon of the whole thing! No real people at all! It was the last straw.

That's why when old Boomers gather, toss back a few beverages, and whine about the old days, many of us contend that the first three *Star Wars* movies, when the real Yoda ruled, were better than the last three because the first three, which are really the second three, came first, even before the final three, not including the three prequels, which are really the first three but were made last. (Boomers understand. Got any more beverages?) Sure, the technology is superb. But remember when they used real actors like Yoda? It's just not the same.

All this illustrates how far we traveled in a very short time. When television replaced the stories of Elders, puppets took over part of the task of educating our young. From Howdy Doody to the Sesame Street gang, puppets gradually became the ones who instructed and entertained our children.

Who evolved into the ultimate instructor? He is now completely digitized. Yoda doesn't even have a cloth body anymore. To paraphrase Papa Vader out of context, "Our training is complete!" Elders have been replaced by disembodied digits. Trust a guy from the dark side to tell it like it is. Right on, Darth!

This detour into silliness has a purpose. My excursion into puppet fantasy is an attempt to illustrate on a different kind of stage how the search for wisdom devolved from the content of actual people's experience to digital symbols on a computer hard drive. That, in a nutshell, is a perfect example of what happened during the decade of the '70s.

Whereas people used to gather together to listen to real people, we now withdraw into individual rooms to converse with an inanimate computer screen. Our computers are clever, like Yoda and his ilk, but at their root they only convey patterns of 1s and 0s that, at best, can convey ideas. But even those ideas are expressed only in words on a screen. They carry none of the living, breathing warmth of a human voice of experience. They are valuable tools and expensive playthings, not Elders.

When a society seeks knowledge at the expense of wisdom, they elevate smart people rather than wise Elders—geeks over philosophers. Admittedly, *knowledge* changes so quickly that it is sometimes difficult for Elders to keep up. *Wisdom*, though, is a long, slow accumulation of ideas and experiences. Knowledge tells you *how* to do things. Wisdom asks whether or not you *should* do them.

"But computers can convey the wisdom of the ages to everyone on Earth!" you insist. "They can put me in touch with wise people of every age, people I might never have heard of before I bought my new laptop."

And you would be right. Your computer *can* do this. But *does* it? Is that how you really use it? And while you are trying to answer that question, consider the "Case of the Vanishing Elder," a phenomenon that began at precisely the same time the exponential, explosive growth of technology began to take over our imagination. Is technology the smoking gun? Did we begin to devalue the wisdom of our Elders at precisely the same time we began to lust after the knowledge of a brave new world? In our thirst to know more and more facts containing less and less substance, did we take a wrong turn in the road? Are our Elders still out there ready to again take their place among us if only we invite them to take their rightful position at the cultural campfire?

Meditate on a few things:

- We have recently witnessed an almost unprecedented number of large corporations--from lending institutions, to churches, to members of the national government--called on the carpet or made to pay huge financial penalties because they have been found guilty of doing things that were illegal, unethical and unwise. *Where were the voices of wisdom?*
- We have recently witnessed nations around the world, including our own, led astray by those who placed political expediency before the common good and have allowed people in power to follow personal agendas rather than consensus-driven avenues of peace. *Where were the voices of wisdom?*
- We have recently seen social systems, ranging from health care to tax structures, bend under the weight of economic forces and moneyed expediency, rather than cultural reform. *Where were the voices of wisdom?*
- We have recently witnessed the highest courts in our land and governing bodies of the most prestigious order scandalized by the actions of their members. *Where were the voices of wisdom?*

My impression is that the voices of wisdom were always there. We just didn't listen. The voices of wisdom were drowned out in our time by the noise and clashing words of some media people who wanted a superficial sound bite rather than a wise conversation. From sea to shining sea, America is blessed with real Elders—people of wisdom, but they are a vanishing breed. So many people are, with each passing day, ignoring wisdom in order to worship at the altar of pragmatic knowledge brought to us by Facebook, Twitter, Google, and their ilk.

What happens when you lose your Elders? What happens when wisdom, passed on from generation to generation, becomes lost? More specifically, what happens when a culture loses its Elders in its lust for technology? What happened to people in past times whose technology advanced faster than their wisdom to control it?

Simply put, their culture died. How many lost civilizations now lie buried beneath the dust of centuries? Are we the next? If so, our downfall can be clearly seen if we study the decade of the '70s.

You can't condense the whole downfall into one ten-year period. As a matter of fact, it began before that and is still going on. But that one decade is a pretty good case study of how it happens. We weren't ready for the computer revolution. Our growth into maturity as a society didn't match our development of technology that brought both riches and disaster. We couldn't handle it all.

And now we are paying the price.

Thus it was that a decade that--for me, at least--began in depression, ended in busy-ness. The American lifestyle puts too much of a burden on our shoulders to allow time for much despair. I have called that decade an age of illusion for good reason.

Stage magicians usually prefer the term "Illusionists." They aren't doing real magic. They are creating illusions. They are keeping your attention occupied over *here,* while deceiving manipulation is going on over *there.* What they are doing isn't real. It's an illusion of reality. But it *seems* so real that we accept it. Sometimes we are even delighted by the deception. We take pleasure in our ability to be deceived. We revel in it.

The '70s were like that in many ways. We knew something real was going on, but in many ways we deliberately embraced the illusion. We paid lip service to the fact that technology was dangerous, but we weren't keeping up with the moral ramifications of it.

We knew it was taking over our lives. We knew we had no way to dispose of nuclear waste, for instance, but we willingly believed the illusionists who told us that when the time came, we would find a way to take care of the problem.

We knew we were despoiling the oceans, but we chose to believe that somebody would do something about it if it got serious.

We knew politicians were becoming ever more corrupt due to the new technology they possessed, but we assumed the right guys could fix it after the next election.

Why didn't we do anything? Well, the truth is, many people tried. There were heroes in the '70s, make no mistake about it. But many more, like me, didn't do much except complain.

Why? First of all, we felt powerless. Second, we were busy just trying to get by. We were faced with great, life-altering changes that everyone has to go through in their twenties, but the social under-pinning had dropped away. America was confused.

It was, for the most part, a generational confusion. The voice of the Elder had been silenced. Sometimes that was the case be-cause the Elders, who should have known better, surrendered their power.

There were some journalists such as Walter Cronkite, Jane Pauley, Lesley Stahl, Andrea Mitchell, Tom Brokaw, and others, who still commanded our respect and attention. Talk show host Dick Cavett and some of his colleagues even kept entertainment at a high intellectual level.

There were many, many more who richly wore the mantel of Elder. By the time the '80s rolled around, those who had eyes to see could, indeed, see the writing on the wall. Things were chang-ing. The Illusion continued well into the next decade. Indeed, it still weaves its spell.

But there were other, home-grown elders who kept things real. I want to take a moment to tell you about one of them. His name was Corser.

Interlude: Corser
The Other Side of the '70s

THE CULTURE

Some things are worth holding on to. They are real in the midst of a great illusion. Corser was real.

Don Corser is a native New Englander who--probably because he spent time in the merchant marine--tends to call people by their last names. I was always Willis to him, so he is, whenever I think about him, Corser.

He was one of the best friends I ever had, the Elder who had the greatest influence on my life. He may be the one rock-solid reality that I experienced during the illusion of the '70s. I say that because the experiences we shared have remained with me throughout the decades that followed, while I have forgotten much of whatever it was that seemed so important during those tumultuous years of change and so-called progress.

He never made the headlines. He won't be written up in any academic analysis of the history of the period. But he came at the very end of a golden age that, like it or not, featured what has come to be known as a uniquely American way of life. I doubt we will ever see it again. It was the age of the authentic American Sportsman. I probably see it now through rose-colored glasses. I doubt it was as pure as I remember it. But if it *didn't* unfold off the reel just the way it now appears on the screen of my memory banks, it *should* have.

To truly appreciate Corser we have to travel first on my road, then his. Only then will our two paths meet and lead us to insights that I hope are eternal.

When I graduated from the Eastman School of Music in Rochester, New York, I expected to be a full-time professional musician, and for a while I was.

But in Rochester I came under the influence of some men who roamed the woods and fields that, before the building boom of the '70s, made up the countryside outside the city. Ben and Ellison, Ken and The Jolly Green Giant, Finley and Cap, all took over where my father had begun, teaching me to hunt, fish, and play the fiddle.

My way of coping with the city for five weekdays was to have someone drop me off in the woods for the weekend. Equipped only with a hunting knife, knapsack, fishing rod, or rifle, I would live off the land for a few days. If I didn't get anything to eat, I went hungry. As a result, I still have fond memories of roast woodchuck for breakfast, cooked slowly over an open fire, with blueberries for dessert. I seem to have conveniently forgotten the days I went without.

Later, when I took up residence in central Massachusetts at the ripe old age of 25 or so, I naturally discovered Corser.

Living off the land — Marion, NY (1970).

He was in his late sixties then. His hunting partner had just died, a loss any real sportsman will understand, so I gravitated into the vacuum.

Corser changed me. Like every kid in his early twenties, I measured the success of a hunting or fishing trip by how much game I brought home, since in my early hunting experience *not* shooting something meant going hungry. Those days, too, our young family had a tradition that the Thanksgiving table could hold only food I shot, caught, or raised. Vegetables from the garden were flanked by a pheasant, a grouse or two, a brace of woodcock on the side, perhaps enhanced by a squirrel or rabbit. The tradition lasted only until the kids got old enough to ask why we couldn't eat turkey like everyone else. It broke my heart, and to this day Thanksgiving is not the same.

So, I was a slash-and-burn hunter. General Sherman himself could have learned something from me. When Corser and I went into the woods, I was accompanied by my favorite dog, Coco; Corser's two shorthaired pointers; a shotgun; and an attitude. The only advantage the wildlife enjoyed was that Corser didn't want to kill anything, and I couldn't. The spirit was willing, but when it came to flying targets, I was a lousy shot. My more liberal, consciousness-raised friends used to say to me, "How can you shoot those poor, innocent birds?" My reply was always the same. "I don't know. How? I try and try and can't hit a thing."

When all three dogs went on point, and a ruffed grouse or pat—New England-ese for partridge—looking at least three feet long, came boiling out of a cover headed for daylight, I sometimes got three shots off into the trees and sky before Corser could yell, "There goes a magnificent specimen of *Bonasa umbellus!*" or some such Latin equivalent. He would then apologize to the dogs for not doing his part, and off we would go again.

Corser's road, you see, had been different from mine. He was old enough to remember the glory years of hunting after the war. World War II had kept hunters overseas long enough for farms to grow into bird Heaven. Brush piles, overgrown fields, and scrub woods, perfect habitat for upland game, had experienced an explosion of birds, so he had long since outgrown his need to hunt for the table. He was in it now for the dogs and the experience.

I never saw him kill a trout. They were always returned to the stream. By then, the native trout population in New England had been pretty much depleted, and he considered the fish stocked by the Fish and Game people to be "pretty poor fodder." On the occasions he did bring down a pat for dinner, I always saw a look in his eyes that revealed his wish to return the bird back to the cover so he could hunt it again. He didn't feel that way about pheasants. They were stocked birds as well. But the woodcock and grouse we hunted were as native as he was. At least the grouse were. Woodcock are migratory. But while in New England, they were home, as far as Corser saw it.

Lee Wulf once said, "A game fish is too valuable to be caught only once." That's how Corser felt. He enjoyed the *act* of hunting and the *act* of fishing, and he could easily be made to pontificate against those who spoiled the essence of the sport.

But to understand that, you have to understand a little about the fishing hierarchy as defined by purist, old-school, trout fishermen.

At the top of the pecking order are those who fly fish. When you catch a trout on a dry fly, you are participating in quite a different experience from those who (horrors!) throw gaudy, metal plugs or, even worse, bait, at lesser fish. So there are *dry fly* fishermen, followed somewhat down the scale by fishermen who fish *wet* with nymphs and streamers below the surface. Then, there are those who *spin fish* with a light line. Then there's nothing for a long way until you reach the bass-boat, crank-bait, bass-casting fraternity. After that, there's nothing at all unless you're a kid with a cane pole who doesn't know any better.

That's why, while gardening peacefully one evening long ago, I heard a screech of brakes, a squealing of tires, and a voice sounding forth across the quiet New England common, "Willis! Was that a worm I saw you pick up out of that compost heap?"

One of my favorite memories of Corser, though, was the night we were fishing from his canoe, way up and gone back in the boon-

Before the attack of the huts. Fishing with Corser.

docks, right at twilight. Neither of us had said a word for what seemed like hours, and I was entranced by the sight of a woodcock sitting on a whacking big hemlock stump with the sun setting right behind him. It was beautiful, quiet, and relaxing.

Then we were attacked by the huts.

Now, to understand what "huts" are you have to know that canoe racing was just getting big in those parts. Two paddlers would race up streams or across lakes, and whenever the man in the stern yelled "Hut!" they would flip their paddles to the other side of the canoe and keep moving.

Corser had a nice float going and I was idly watching the woodcock when we heard, "Hut!" (splash, splash, splash) "Hut!" (splash, splash, splash), and around the bend came a racing canoe headed right for us. I was in the bow, facing away from Corser, so I didn't see his face when the lead paddler yelled, "Excuse me, sir. We're coming through!"

Corser yanked his line out of the water, getting it tangled in a tree behind him, and we watched the racing canoe ram the beaver dam up-river from us, then back off and ram it again. When it became obvious that they weren't going to get over or through it, they turned around right in front of us and headed back down the river.

I didn't dare turn around and look at Corser. I just sat there, waiting.

Corser didn't say a word.

I heard him reel in his line and pick up a paddle.

I did the same.

The silence grew profound.

I still didn't dare say a word.

After about ten minutes Corser said, very quietly, "Hut!"

I almost fell out of the boat.

Next day Corser ran his pickup truck into the yard, came to a screeching halt, and yelled, "Willis! There's hen huts too! I just saw a hatch coming off the river!"

Translation: He had seen some women racers from the bridge downstream from where we were fishing the night before.

That's Corser. Some of the greatest times of my life were spending October days with him in the Adirondacks, hunting in

Bass Fishing in the Adirondacks (mid-1980s).

the morning and fishing in the afternoon. (Bass fishing. Corser wasn't quite a purist when he wasn't in New England.)

But what I will ever be thankful for was a vision he showed me one morning. I think he had quietly put up with my bird-lust sinfulness until he sensed I was ready for conversion. It was early winter, and we were hunting pats. I think Corser liked January hunting best. Pheasant season, when we chased those gaudy Korean imports, was closed and the woodcock had all gone south, so we were forced to be purists. Bird hunting meant partridge hunting, and that was as it should be.

All fall he had warned me I was moving too fast, missing the apples that were growing--that year, at least--on the ancient trees planted back who-knows-when by old timers who had long since killed their last partridge. Stone cellar holes marked the place where their dreams of forever had come to an end, but lilies-of-the-valley still graced the sites of old kitchen gardens in the spring.

It was a warm day right in the middle of the January thaw, and we had walked up into the woods until we came to a magnificent view of the valley far below. There, Corser proceeded to sit down on a stump in the middle of a cut-over and lean his unfired gun against a tree.

I did the same thing.

Eventually, the dogs got the idea we weren't doing anything serious that day, so they went to sleep.

I've mostly forgotten what we talked about, but I seem to remember covering a huge amount of philosophical territory. We started with people who used to live in our town and then moved on to topics like the environment being paved or built up. Then we covered differences between New Englanders and everybody else before moving on to religion. Corser was good at quoting Scripture. "As ye sow, so shall ye reap!" was a favorite. A lot of old timers who had passed on were skewered with that one.

Eventually, though, he looked at me and said, "Well, do you suppose we've stayed here long enough so we can go home now?"

Cosmo and Me

I must have looked surprised. "Aren't we going hunting?"

Corser looked at me. "Willis, you've got to understand that sometimes hunting has nothing at all to do with shooting birds!"

Aha! A vista opened before me. I guess I was ready to see, for the first time in my life, what hunting and fishing were really all about. I can't explain it to you. That would be as silly as trying to explain Grand Canyon to a person from New Jersey. You don't explain vistas. You simply experience them.

All I know is that from that time on I very rarely killed birds, and I spent a lot of time looking for old apple trees. I started hiking more and hunting less.

Now, please understand. I'm not anti-hunt and anti-gun. I want to see future generations come to know the same experience I had. I don't consider myself holier-than-thou when it comes to field sports, and I don't have a lot of patience with the rather shallow views expressed by those who claim to be ecologically minded but have never been in a by-God wilderness and don't know the difference between a Labrador retriever and a black duck.

But I consider my evolution from hunter/gatherer to agriculturalist to city-dwelling preacher to nature-loving appreciator a sacred journey, as well as a microcosm of human history. That day with Corser, I saw the vista at the end of the road. I began to *feel*, not just *know*, that life is about traveling, not arriving. Bringing home the prize is not the object; it's merely the excuse for being out there doing it.

I exist as a part of the world. That's easy to say. Many people do. Most think they really believe it. But to experience it in the very fiber of your being you need to see the vista. And although I don't want to sound melodramatic, perhaps that is the very vista that will lead us 21st techno-buffs to the Promised Land.

The vista I saw because of Corser effectively closed one door and opened another. My life took a sudden turn. Spending less time chasing after critters gave me more time to hit the books. I turned inward and began to develop my career as a minister. But the memories continued to remain fresh and clear, much more focused than whatever else happened in those long-ago decades.

They still do. Here are just a few that shaped my life during the '70s and '80s, when I was privileged to spend time with Corser.

THE QUESTION

Illusions fade over time. The memories of my best friend only grow stronger. So where do we find the real reality in this game called life?

Springtime in New England is as about as good as it gets. You have to take advantage of it because it only lasts for about two and a half hours between snow melt and the arrival of the black flies, followed by mosquitoes, and then ending up with a plague of the biggest, fiercest, and most blood-sucking critters you ever saw: horseflies. They last until first frost in September, so when spring arrives, you'd better take advantage of it and go trout fishing. The water is cold in the streams and brooks. A few hours before, most of it was snow. But a good pair of waders and a newly waxed fly line go a long way toward warming up the cockles of a true sportsman's heart.

There was a day in the early '70s when spring arrived at about 7:00 one fine morning early in the week and not on a Saturday. When spring comes on Saturday, you have to watch out because the water will be crammed with fishermen. But Corser was retired, and I was somewhat able to arrange my own schedule, so when it broke on a Tuesday or Wednesday, we had more elbow room.

Knowing what was coming, I had already put my fishing gear in shape and patched up my waders, a chore I always promised I would attend to during the cold days of January but never quite seemed to get around to. This year was an exception. During a false alarm in early March, I had accomplished the task early, so I was ready when the phone rang.

"Willis! Are your waders ready to go or are you about to get wet?"

"I'm ready," I said with a certain aura of smug.

"Make enough coffee for two. I'm on my way! And this time don't forget the doughnuts!"

He'll never let me forget the time I thought I had met every contingency but the one he considered to be of prime importance. The nearest store was ten miles away, but I had felt this coming a few days ago, so I was ready when he drove into my driveway and helped me sling things aboard his truck.

This year I had added a new weapon to my arsenal. Alarmed at how much hand-tied dry flies had risen in price, I had determined to tie my own, aided by a Christmas present from my wife. She had bought me a small fly-tying kit, complete with hackle, thread, portable vice, an assortment of hooks, and an instruction book. I had not yet proceeded to the level of skill needed to tie the kind of masterful renditions Corser used.

It wasn't that I didn't have any of my own. I had the good fortune of being friends with the wife of Corser's old fishing buddy. He had passed away before we met, but she had given me his old assortment of flies, carefully placed in boxes sorted according to wet, dry, and streamers. I still have them, as a matter of fact, fifty years later. They're much too pretty to actually use.

(Even back in those days a good dry fly sold for a buck or more. Corser used to tell a story about the day his partner had dropped a box on the kitchen floor while packing up one morning, spilling the contents all over the room.

"Kenneth," his partner's wife had said. "Do you need so many? They must be expensive!"

"They sure are!" Ken had replied with a straight face. "Some of those cost ten cents apiece!")

But this year I wanted to do it on my own. Corser had never learned to tie his own flies, and I wanted to show off. Okay, maybe I wanted to impress him. He was, after all, a bit of a father figure.

Although I was still a beginner, I had learned to tie up some presentable Mickey Finns. Those are streamers designed to resemble small minnows. You fish them below the surface, even downstream, and they can be worked without nearly the finesse required to fish dry flies on top. In other words, a klutz like me can slash around and actually catch a fish or two, as long as they're not too sophisticated.

We headed to our favorite stream that flowed through a bird cover we used to call the Chicken Coop. There was a bridge near the place we put in, and one of us would fish upstream and the other down. While en route, Corser carefully instructed me what flies to use and how to present them to maximum effect.

God forgive me, I cut him off.

"I don't think so," I said. "I tied up some streamers and thought I'd use them downstream from the bridge, right up to the big hole. I see fresh rainbow trout on my dinner plate tonight."

There was dead silence from the driver's side of the truck.

"You tied up some streamers?" he said with disbelief.

"Yeah. Something I've been working on."

"Let's see 'em."

I opened up my streamer box and showed him my master-pieces.

"Did you bring a net?" he asked.

"Why?" I replied.

"So you can scoop the fish out of the water when they laugh themselves to death!"

That did it. I was now on a mission. Corser was going to be impressed on this beautiful spring day.

We hit the bridge, geared up, drank some coffee, had a dough-nut, and separated—he to employ his considerable skill in luring native brook trout to the top, me to plunge into the depths of a dark rift of water in search of the elusive rainbow trout that had probably been recently planted by the Fish and Game folks.

His last words to me were, "Please don't tell anyone you know me. It's bad enough that you're a preacher. But to fish streamers? You might as well use a cane pole and a bobber."

Never the less, I persevered.

"Please!" was my retort. "I have my good reputation to uphold."

"You're a fisherman, Willis, so you don't have a good reputation!"

Moving quietly downstream, I probed the banks and riffles for about a hundred yards. I had a few hits, but nothing I could call substantial. Just before I reached the big hole, an area where the stream opened up into some deep water that almost looked like a small pond, I found what I was looking for. The water swirled around a big rock that stood about a foot or so out from an overhanging bank. If I was a rainbow trout, that's where I would hide, waiting for a bait fish to swim by.

It looked perfect. My hands started to shake, and it wasn't just from the cold. A few fishermen stood below the hole, politely watching me, not wanting to spoil my approach. In those days, there was etiquette involved in being an outdoorsman.

I stood for a minute or so, planning my presentation. You can't rush these things. I studied the water and figured out just what I would do. If I were to let out a little more line than needed, I could put the streamer just about a foot upstream from the slack water. Then, a little shake of the rod to make the line land in a series of "S" loops so as to produce some slack. The streamer would be carried right into the hole, and I could give it a little twitch as soon as the line straightened out. It would look just like a small bait fish, struggling against the current. Any self-respecting rainbow trout would pounce, hungry or not. It would be too good to resist.

For once, everything worked out perfectly. The streamer landed in just the right place to be carried by the current. I had estimated the amount of line I needed right to the inch. I twitched the streamer at just the right time. I was so happy with the presentation that it never occurred to me I might actually catch a trout.

But—there it was! Ka-boom! Right on cue. I was so surprised I forgot to set the hook, but the fish had hit with such explosive power that it hooked itself. Flying about a foot out of the water and shaking his tail, the fight was on. Somehow, he had made a tactical error. He had come out of his jump on my side of the rock and headed for the big water where I could play him. There are times when it's better to be lucky than good. I stumbled a few feet to a more advantageous position where I could give him some room to tire himself out. Then it was just a matter of fish versus fisherman.

This was the biggest fish I had ever had on a fly rod. We fought each other for what must have been all of ten or fifteen minutes. I couldn't rein him in without risk of breaking the leader. All I could do was hold on and try not to do anything foolish.

I was dimly aware that a small crowd of fishermen--maybe half a dozen or so—had gathered on the bank of the hole. Advice came thick and fast.

"Give him line!"

"Don't give him too much line!"

"Let him run!"

"Hold him in!"

"Keep your rod tip up!"

"Lower your rod tip!"

After a long time, I felt him beginning to tire. Slowly, very slowly, I maneuvered myself so I could slide him carefully up on the mud beach, where I was able to grab him behind the gills and lift him clear of the water.

The small crowd burst into applause. A job well done. I had never felt prouder. In my mind's eye, he was about three feet long and weighed about ten pounds, but I think 18 inches and slightly north of a couple of pounds is closer to the truth. On the other hand, if I hadn't taken him, he would have grown a lot bigger by now, so every time I think about him, he gains a little length and weight. It's not exactly lying. That's just how fishermen think.

I fished for a while longer, but my heart wasn't in it. I was too jazzed up. My only wish was that Corser could have seen it. That would show him! But things being as they were, I decided to make my way back to the truck.

On the way, I met a guy coming back down the path who said, "Hey, do you know the guy fishing upstream? I met him just now on my way to checking in with my buddy to tell him that streamers are the way to go today. I told him about your fish. He just looked at me and said, 'Young guy with a beard and glasses?'

"I said, 'That's the one.' Funny thing, the old guy acted like he knew you but didn't say a thing."

So! He knew! I was now famous. This was going to be good!

As I approached the truck with my prize, there was Corser, leaning on the hood.

I didn't say a thing. Just plopped my fish down on the tailgate.

Corser looked at me, looked at the fish, and said, "Just the one?"

The memories keep coming, more vivid than ever, more real than even my present-day experience.

One bright January day back in the 1970s, I awoke to a two-inch skim of fresh snow on the ground, a beautiful blue New England sky overhead, and the temperatures promising an almost spring-like day ahead. Even before I sat down to breakfast, I knew what would happen. Sure enough, the phone rang. It was Corser.

"Willis!" he shouted, using his most commanding voice. "I don't care what you've got going today. We're going hunting!" And he hung up the phone.

This being January, it meant that we were hunting pats that day. As I said earlier, this was Corser's favorite kind of hunting because the big, glamour seasons such as pheasant and deer were behind us. That meant only dedicated grouse hunters such as ourselves would take to the woods. We rarely saw anyone on these days. It also meant we would take our dogs with us, and Corser lived to watch the dogs work. We rarely shot anything, but that was fine.

An occasional dinner of partridge, pheasant, or woodcock was appreciated but no longer necessary for him. Put that together with a skim of fresh tracking snow and he was in Heaven.

(Or only partially in Heaven. I once asked him what his idea of Heaven was. He thought for a moment and then said, in complete seriousness, "Heaven will be a place where for six months of the year you get up every morning to find a perfect day for hunting pats with the perfect dog. The dog never misses a point and you never miss a shot. When he brings the bird back to your hand, you release it, and it flies away free.

Then, for the other six months of the year, you wake up to a perfect day to fish for native brook trout in a perfect stream. You hit every rise, catch every fish, and release it to fish some more."

"Then what's Hell?" I asked.

"Hell," he said, "is when the seasons overlap and you have to decide which one you're going to do that day!")

This day was definitely made in Heaven, and it wasn't long before I had whistled up my German Shorthaired Pointer, Coco, took my grandfather's old shotgun off the rack (the one reserved for only perfect days!), and drove to Corser's house to meet up with his two pointers and the chairman of the board, Corser himself.

"Willis," he announced, "You're a history buff. Today I'm going to show you a piece of history—something you've never seen before."

Little did we know how right he was.

We took off through the woods, Corser and I, along with three very eager dogs. Our destination that day had nothing to do with grouse. He wanted to show me an old cellar hole, where a forgotten pioneer's homestead once stood. These places dot the New England woods. They mark the place where a determined dreamer once built a house he thought would last forever. Often, sad to say, such places are surrounded by a private cemetery where the man's family succumbed to sickness, accident, childbirth complications, or any of the host of misfortunes that plague life just a little beyond the leading edge of civilization.

Usually, the only thing that evoked historical memories was an easily missed hole in the ground built up with dry-stone foundation walls above which a long-forgotten family laughed, cried, ate, slept, and labored together. At the proper time of year, you sometimes found a flourishing bed of lily-of-the-valley that had been planted by a long-forgotten housewife who looked for beauty where others saw only hardship.

On this January day, flowers were only a glimmer on the far horizon of spring, but, as we approached the old homestead, I fell into my usual musings. Who were these people? What were they looking for? How did they get by? What were their hopes and unfulfilled dreams? Am I looking at the view that greeted them outside their door every morning? Why did they settle here? What caused them to leave? Death? Sickness? Indians? Despair?

As always, I tried to get inside their heads.

Then it happened, and I'll never forget it.

All three dogs suddenly stopped, sat back on their haunches, and let out a long, drawn-out wail. These were bird dogs. They never howled like hounds. But each of them was visibly shaking and acted terrified.

Coco crawled to what he considered safety behind me. All three dogs stared intently at the cellar hole and pressed up against us. They wouldn't move.

Corser looked at me and mouthed the word, "Bear?" It was a question, not a statement.

But what would a bear be doing up and around at this time of year? No self-respecting, hibernating bear would be out yet, even if the day did feel like spring.

Just to be sure, we walked a wide circle around the old homestead. Tracking was easy. The virgin snow was fresh and lay in an undisturbed and even layer all around. We moved out farther and looked some more. Nothing. Whatever spooked the dogs had left no tracks.

We checked the trees, wondering if some kind of bird was nesting nearby. But these were bird dogs. They wouldn't have been this terrified if a whole flock of turkeys, a score of vultures, and a goose or two were staring down at them.

Suddenly the dogs got up, shook themselves in unison, and moved out again as if nothing had happened. They were fine.

But we weren't.

"What the Hell was that about?" said Corser.

I had no answer. But we both had seen the hair on our dog's necks standing up stiff. We had both experienced something that made our skin crawl We both knew we had been in the presence of something real enough to frighten the wits out of our companions, who had obviously sensed something neither of us could.

"Always trust your dog!"

Corser had drummed that into my head a hundred times.

"They sense things you can't. Believe them! If they say something is in the bush, it is!"

And now this. What were we to think? What had they sensed that we couldn't find any evidence for?

I think that even back then I knew the answer to that question. Spiritually, I knew we had been in the presence of something beyond our normal perception. Now I'm sure of it, but back then I was an intellectual agnostic bordering on skepticism when it came to metaphysical matters. There is no doubt in my mind that the old homesteader was still around on that day. He may have left no tracks, but he was out there, just beyond our ability to perceive him. He was watching us. The dogs knew. And I trusted them.

Over the years I have refined a group of sayings that stand out in my mind. I call them "Corser-isms." If life is a moving picture, these are slides that stand still, thus framing and illuminating an incident—or perhaps it would be better called a pattern of reality—that defined my friend Corser.

I better explain what I mean by that statement. It will take an illustration or two.

Corser was frugal in a good way. He had learned economic discipline during the Great Depression. He wasn't cheap by any means. He just had a healthy respect for value and a very low BS quotient toward anyone who tried to take advantage of him.

I don't know if it still happens, but the biggest sportsman's show in New England used to take place outside of Boston once a year. I had never attended one, but Corser decided we needed to go and check it out, so he dutifully showed up one morning and we trundled off to become city sportsmen for the day.

We were not disappointed in that regard. Corser immediately picked up on the fact that many of the thousands of attendees probably considered the Boston Common to be real wilderness. He had a very low threshold of patience for such folks. I well remember the day a city-type fellow screeched to a halt in front of us one day when we were exiting a cover that had produced nary a single point by any of our three dogs. That didn't bother us any. We weren't in it just for the birds. But when the guy appeared to be almost apoplectic, Corser said, *sotto voce*, "He's going to tell us he just saw a pheasant cross the road."

As the guy rolled down his window he yelled, "Are you guys huntahs?" (This was, after all, New England.)

Corser looked at me, then looked down at himself and the gun he was carrying, and said, "Well, we've got the clothes."

The guy was so excited he didn't get it. So rather than think before he spoke, he shouted out, "There's a house about a half mile back on the road with a bird bath on the front lawn." (The house was Corser's.) "There's a ruffled grouse right in the middle of the lawn!" (That's right. He said "ruffled.")

Corser looked at me and then said, with a perfectly straight face, "Thank you, sir. We'll report it right away."

The guy just looked at us, rolled up his window and drove off.

Anyway, when we disembarked onto the show grounds and saw the corduroy elbow patches, the jaunty hats complete with feathers, and what looked like a showroom full of L. L. Bean models, I knew it would just be a matter of time.

Corser did pretty well throughout the morning, but by lunchtime we were feeling a mite peckish. Hungry, too. We had spent a half hour watching a fly-casting demonstration, listening to a guy pontificate about how we could all be better casters if we would just buy more expensive equipment, which, thank goodness, he could sell us at a discount for today only. Corser's comment was that the dude could cast, but he probably couldn't fish.

With starvation only a few moments away, we exited the main hall and found our way to the snack concession. There was a big sign advertising "Ham sandwiches — $6.50." (Remember, this was the '70s. $6.50 still could buy two tanks of gas.)

Corser stood in line for a few minutes until we reached the front, then said, in a very loud voice, "Let me see one of those $6.50 ham sandwiches!"

The guy behind the counter reached down and pulled out some wax paper that contained two pieces of standard white bread, a thin piece of processed ham, and a limp piece of lettuce. Corser unwrapped it and looked it over.

"That'll be $6.50," said the vendor.

"Oh, I didn't want to *buy* one. I said I just wanted to *see* it," said Corser. And then walked away. He could be succinct in his criticisms when he wanted to be.

You might wonder whether such traits are naturally occurring or taught. I tend to believe it's the former. In other words, Corser was probably born that way—a master of understatement when he wanted to be. I think it ran in his family.

One year he did some major renovation on his house and discovered some really bad fire damage behind the wall near the chimney area. The whole thing was charred beyond repair and had to be completely replaced. We marveled that the house had survived.

"That explains it," said Corser, and went upstairs to retrieve a journal written by either his mother or grandmother, I forgot which. He lived in a house his ancestors had built just before they hiked west to fight the Revolutionary War Battle of Bennington, got there two days too late, and so hiked home. It was an old house!

But in the journal was a short, rather cryptic entry: "Had to put out a chimney fire today." That was it. No big deal. A Corser-ism way before his time.

Corser-isms also revealed the boy that still lived in the man. Once, when we were coming out of a pheasant cover, a hunting party arrived on the scene to hunt the cover we had just finished with. Four people piled out of the truck, one of them a very pretty young woman who toted her shotgun as if she knew how to use it. She smiled a big smile at Corser and said, "Did you leave any for us?"

"We left all of them," said Corser.

We then proceeded to watch as they assembled their gear, called out their dogs, and headed into the brush. Just before they disappeared, she turned and said, again to Corser, and again with a big smile, "Thanks! We appreciate it!"

Corser just stood there until they had gone, and then said, rather wistfully, "There was something we used to do with them. But I forgot what it was."

That might explain his story about passing through the Panama Canal while he was in the Merchant Marine. The boat pulled into a lock and for a few minutes was still reachable by the vendors who lined the walls, hoping to sell things to the rich Americans onboard before they sank down to the next level. One such entrepreneur corralled Corser and yelled, "Sir! May I sell you some immoral pictures?"

Corser looked up at him and said, "I've been at sea for six months. Can I sell *you* some immoral pictures?"

He was definitely a man of his times, though. The values that he held as a child stayed with him throughout life. He once caught me walking over to the Post Office on a rainy day. I was carrying an umbrella.

"Willis! What are you doing? Real men don't use umbrellas."

He told me that when, as a kid, his mother insisted he take one with him to school, he would hide it in the bushes as soon as he was out of sight of the house.

But then, one day, while studying the journals of Lewis and Clark written during their famous expedition of discovery, I learned that William Clark was distraught one day to realize he had lost his bumbershoot. I immediately showed the passage to Corser. He wouldn't believe it, convinced as he was that I was practicing a kind of revisionist history and destroying one of his heroes.

"'Bumbershoot' must have meant something different back then."

Corser had a total respect for history. For the first three years I hunted with him, he took me to all his favorite bird covers, most of which he had been hunting since he was a kid. I really appreciated the gesture. For those of you who don't understand grouse hunting, bird covers are cloaked in secrecy to those outside of the fraternity. They are given code names and jealously guarded. We hunted "Five Points," "Sally's Backhouse," the "Chicken Coop," both north and south, and the "Mill," but never revealed their whereabouts to anyone, checking constantly to make sure we weren't being followed on our way in.

Other bird hunters knew about these covers, of course. But they had their own names and thought, as we did, that no one knew about them. We would sometimes come across spent shotgun shells and a cigarette butt or two at the entrance but would usually pretend they could be explained by more prosaic reasons.

One day, when we had struck out at the more productive covers, Corser announced, "Okay, that does it. We're going to hunt the

Widow _____'s Mowing." (To tell you the truth, I've forgotten the widow's name.)

This was a new one for me. I was excited.

"Let's go," I said, ready to discover a new cover that he had never showed me. Unexplored covers offer the best hunting by far.

We drove to an unnamed location we had hunted before. It was a fine stand of trees, some of them forty or fifty years old. I was very familiar with it, but assumed we just needed to penetrate through the timber before we reached the mowing.

That morning, we again stayed in the trees. No mowing was to be found.

Growing impatient, I asked, "Where's the mowing?"

"You're in it!" he said with great exasperation. It hadn't been mowed for 40 or 50 years, but it was still the Widow _____'s Mowing. That's what happens when you live with one foot firmly rooted in your past. The more I think about it, the more I realize that's not a bad way to live.

As I have implied over and over again, it's a mistake to think that a real sportsman is simply interested in bringing home game or fish. That's the *excuse* for going. It's not the *reason*. Thus it is that Corser had strict rules about ethics when it came to bringing down the prey that we sought. One of the strictest was this: If I had ever shot a game bird out of a tree or on the ground, I would have been dumped like a hot potato, branded a "game hog" or worse. A game bird had to be in the air. Period. No excuses. This, by the way, is the root of the expression "a sitting duck." There's simply no challenge in shooting a duck that is motionless on the water. You just don't do it. If you do and are caught in the act, your reputation sinks below that of even Richard Nixon.

That being said, there was one time—and only one—when Corser came close to breaking his own code of conduct.

I like holidays, but the one that I considered for many years to be absolutely sacrosanct was the first week of October. That week doesn't appear as a holiday on *your* calendar, but for many years it was on *mine*.

Corser and his wife owned a small cottage in New York's Adirondack Mountains. During the first week of October, the most glorious time of the year up there, the pheasant, grouse, and woodcock season were all open at the same time. So was the bass season. For a reasonable amount of money, I could get an out-of-state sportsman's license that entitled me to both hunt and fish for three days. My wife and I would drive up on the last day of September, buy a license en route, and stay with the Corsers for three days, driving home the day after my license expired. We would hunt birds all morning and fish all afternoon. The women would explore and hike while we men folk were engaged in our own outdoor pursuits. (What I wouldn't have given to be in on their conversations concerning grown men acting like children! Or, even better, to have been with them the day they explored a small gauge railroad that zig-zagged up a mountain, only to discover when they reached the top and looked down that a bear was following their route up!)

Since all three game bird seasons were open at the same time, our goal every year was to celebrate our final dinner together with something we called "Three-Species Pie." Pheasant, woodcock, and grouse would all be featured in a thick gravy with vegetables of all kinds and whatever else might be available in the kitchen, covered with a thin, flaky, melt-in-your-mouth pastry that only Corser's wife could make. To this day, my mouth waters whenever I think about it. It was different every year, but always the best game dinner I had ever enjoyed. The only thing missing was a fine glass of Chablis. Corser, a recovered alcoholic for 25 years, kept a dry camp. The food was so good, however, that it didn't bother me.

But what do you do when time is running out and you only have two species to put in the three species pie? Grouse were running thin that year. They are a cyclical species anyway, and that year they were few and far between. Okay, so we missed a few as well. Might as well be honest.

That year we were hunting with one of Corser's neighbors. He was great guy who lived full time in the Adirondacks. He was deer hunter, primarily, so when we were out hunting birds and he would say, "Hunting season starts in three weeks," Corser would look at me and say, "What does he think we're doing now?" Aside from that he was a good guy. But this year we had no grouse for the pie, and we were on our way home on the final day.

Suddenly, Corser's friend yelled, "Stop the truck!" He had seen a grouse sitting on a spruce branch right by the side of the road. I sensed trouble coming. Corser's ethics were about to be tested. If he shot the grouse off the tree limb while not in flight, he would be guilty of breaking his rules of engagement. But if the grouse were to fly, the spruce was so thick we'd never have a shot.

At such times I have learned that doing and saying nothing is sometimes the wisest course of action. I wasn't about to contribute to Corser's moral downfall. He was grown man. Let him figure it out.

I could almost see the wheels turning in his head as he contemplated a full complement for three species pie versus a life-time of scruples. Slowly, without disturbing the grouse, who was no doubt taunting Corser while representing a lifetime of his feathered but departed brethren and sistren, a veritable serpent in the wilderness of Corser's Eden, Corser unsheathed his shotgun, quietly inserted two shells, and said, "Willis, yell 'pull.' And if it moves a feather, he's air-born!"

Whispering quietly, saving my best skeet-shooting voice for the culminating command, I said, "On three. One, two, three ..."

I never got to "Pull." Right on three, Corser's gun boomed once, and the bird fell to the ground in a heap of feathers. Our three-species pie was salvaged, brought back into existence from the very depths of despair. But at what cost to Corser's soul?

"Hey!" I said. "I never said 'pull.'"

"I saw him move," Corser exclaimed. "He was just about to go. Go get him for me, will you?"

I walked over and picked up the bird.

"You can dress him out as soon as we get home."

I think Corser didn't want any more to do with that bird. It had, after all, led him straight to perdition. But I might be wrong. Maybe he had seen some indication that escaped me. I was willing, for the sake of our friendship, to give him the benefit of the doubt. Frankly, I was just glad the three-species tradition was intact. I was already thinking about dinner. Nothing more was said about it, but Corser seemed quieter than usual on the rest of the drive home.

That night we were joined for dinner by Corser's friend and his wife. The conversation was animated around the table as the six of us recalled elements of the hunt over the last three days. At the conclusion, before apple pie and ice cream, Corser's friend related the specifics of what we had just consumed with such great relish.

"Yep. Two pheasants, from the 'Big-Sky Country' cover, eight woodcock from the river bottom...."

I couldn't help myself as I chimed in, singing, "... and a partridge in a pear tree." Honestly, it just popped out. I hadn't thought about it in advance. But Corser shot me a withering glance.

"That's enough of that," he growled. We never brought it up again.

A good day's hunt (left to right: Bill Rose, Dick Stone, Jim Willis).

Corser had his mischievous side. I could never really get angry at him for it, but he managed to pull off some pretty outlandish stunts. There was the time, for instance, when he found two abandoned puppies along the side of the road while driving into town one day. Being Corser—a dog man if ever there was one—he had to stop and pick them up. But because he was Corser, he didn't want to raise a couple of un-pedigreed mutts, either. He solved the problem as only he could. A mile closer to town, he spotted a young man on foot whose name was Geoff and who was a member of my church youth group, so he stopped to pick him up. With a perfectly straight face he asked Geoff to do him a favor.

"I'm delivering these pups to the preacher and the woman across the street from him. The white one goes to Mrs. Cole. The black hunting dog goes to Willis. It's a surprise; don't tell them they're from me."

Geoff was glad to oblige, and as soon as he exited the truck with the two dogs, one under each arm, Corser quickly drove away for parts unknown.

The white dog really landed on his feet. Katherine Cole was a very rich lady who lived in New York City and summered in our town. Suffice it to say that the dog enjoyed the best of both worlds, lacked for nothing, and lived a life of privilege to a ripe old age. When he finally died, he was replaced by four of our cats, but that's another story.

The black dog lived with us. His name became Matthew, and his favorite pastime was running down to the local dairy, rolling in the spilled, stale milk, and then coming home and proudly shaking himself dry in our kitchen, extremely proud of himself. As for being a "hunting" dog, he would run cowering from the room if I even glanced at my shotgun. His only redeeming feature was that he was a very lovable dog, and my wife adored him. I'm still not sure why, though.

It was a full two years before I discovered what had happened and who was behind the whole scheme. By then, it was too late. Matthew was a fixture in our household, bad habits and all.

Just because Corser hunted birds and fished for trout didn't mean he hadn't done his share of alternative activities afield. He had hunted deer all his life, being a child of the Depression and the days when not bringing in some venison from time to time meant going hungry. But he had pretty much stopped by the time I knew him. The only deer I ever knew him to harvest was a medium-sized buck that decimated his garden one year. Corser put up with him until the first day of deer season, when he looked out his kitchen window and spotted him sneaking out of the woods to gorge himself on some winter rye Corser had planted to till in come spring, thus adding tilth to the soil. Quietly unsheathing his gun, he went out back of the garage and downed him with one shot through the heart, whereupon he called me and asked if I wanted to go deer hunting with him.

I hadn't planned on it that day, but I was so surprised, I accepted. I had never been deer hunting with Corser and didn't want to waste the opportunity, so I changed my clothes, made a few phone calls to free up my schedule for the morning, got my gear together, and headed for his house.

By the time I got there an hour had passed. "Willis," he said. "I couldn't wait all morning, so I started without you. I've got one down on the ground back of the house. Will you be so kind as to string him up and gut him out for me? I'll help you, but my back gives me fits on these cold days. Don't worry, I made sure he was close to a convenient tree for you. Help yourself to a venison steak for your trouble."

His wife later told me the real story.

But the next year, on opening day, I finally convinced him that due to his success of a year ago he should make it up to me by going out with me on opening day. He said deer hunting was too cold, too solitary, and too sedentary. He wasn't interested. But for my sake he would make the effort this year. He even concocted a fool-proof plan. Across the road from his house, he owned a great piece of timberland that we often hunted during partridge season. There was an old woods road running the length of it that was just overgrown enough to be great bird habitat.

"Get here early before first light," he said. "Don't come to the house. We don't want to disturb any deer that might be close. Just walk out the road until you get to the place where there's a fallen birch tree.

I knew it well.

"Head down about 50 yards and stand in the slash from that old oak grove. I'll start out from the house and drive a deer right to you. Be ready! Stay alert. He's a sneaky one!"

Come the morning, I was ready. It was cold. About 15 degrees or lower. But I was ready to make the sacrifice. In those days, I was dedicated, and this sounded like a perfect plan from the old expert.

It must have been 5:00 in the morning when I quietly drove into Corser's dooryard, snaked out my gun, and fortified myself with a cup of coffee. I didn't want to drink any in the woods. The smell of fresh coffee may wake me up, but it would drive away any self-respecting deer.

Long before the sun rose, I had hiked out the old woods road, turned off at the birch tree, and found a good stand in the old oak slash. There I made myself as comfortable as anyone can be in 15-degree weather and waited.

Dawn came with no deer. 8:00 passed, then 9:00. I was now cold and stiff and had just about given up, but then I saw Corser coming up the hill. He was moving carefully from tree to tree, watching ahead intently. He was so quiet and moving with such stealth that I just knew there was a deer ahead of him, somewhere between him and me.

Now I was alert.

Any deer hunter will tell you what adrenaline will do to you when you know the moment of truth will soon arrive. I searched carefully between the trees and in every little dip between Corser and me. I couldn't see the deer, but I knew he must be close. Corser was now moving from tree to tree, keeping out of sight as much as possible. Time stood still, but it must have been close to 10:30.

Finally, Corser worked himself to a position behind a tree about 20 feet away. Still no deer that I could see. Corser peeked out from behind his cover and whispered, "Willis!"

"Yeah," I said, just as quietly.

"Are we having fun yet?"

It was a dangerous game he was playing. After all, I had a loaded gun.

I wasn't only involved with Corser over sports afield. He was in church every Sunday morning, and usually commented on my sermon at some point during the week, so I knew he was listening.

One year it was voted by the Board of Trustees that it was time to change the carpets in the Sanctuary. To save money, people were asked to show up on a Saturday morning to help remove the

"Are we having fun yet?" — *Waiting for Corser (mid-1980s).*

old, ragged, and rather bedraggled floor covering that hadn't seen much attention for many, many years.

On the appointed day, quite a few parishioners showed up to accomplish the task. They spread out among the pews in groups of three of four and the job was commencing rather well when Corser showed up to lend a hand. In typical fashion, though, he couldn't just walk in and quietly begin work. That wasn't his style. He announced himself as soon as he came through the front door. Glancing around the busy room, he said in quite a loud voice, "I haven't seen this many people on their knees in here since the hurricane back in '38!"

Those who knew Corser laughed. The rest just looked a little bewildered. But soon after this took place, he revealed the depths of his friendship in a way that I will never forget and will forever appreciate.

To put it mildly, our lives were never again the same, and my family was turned upside down, when my wife, Judy, was told she had breast cancer. Eventually, after nine years of valiant living, she finally succumbed to it.

At first, we didn't prepare for her death. We prepared for her to live, and it was a challenge. Back in the '70s, research hadn't progressed as far as it has today. About the only plan of attack was radical surgery and lots of chemotherapy. We had been married back then for almost ten years. We were musicians together, singing and playing for every kind of function imaginable. We had produced two record albums of gospel music. She was the bass player in my band. We had two young kids, who were then just preparing to enter school. Neither one of us had hit 40, and death didn't yet seem a reality.

We had no medical insurance at the time, and I was forced to go to her surgeon, hat in hand, promising to pay him somehow, although at the time I didn't know how. I was very afraid he would refuse to operate, knowing he wouldn't get any money.

But things seemed to work out. There was some question as to whether or not all the cancer was removed after the operation, but we were told it might take five years to find out. That seems like a long time when you're in your thirties. The chemotherapy was rough, but we got through it. For Christmas that year, we received a canceled bill from our doctor. That certainly built up our faith in the goodness of humanity.

It seemed at the time as though we had dodged a bullet. Only much later would we learn we were mistaken. Our cure was to prove to be only a reprieve, but the experience made me appreciate Corser.

![Jim & Judy promotional poster. Photo of Judy (left) and Jim holding a guitar (right).]

MUSIC THAT LIVES /

Jim & Judy

TRADITIONAL AND CONTEMPORARY GOSPEL MUSICIANS

Jim Willis — recent pastor; youth worker and dynamic
bible teacher, brings a vital evangelistic message

Music that lives! (Jim and Judy, 1968–1986).

Not that it had anything to do with hunting and fishing. I wouldn't, even for a moment, want to give the idea that I'm trivializing something as serious as cancer. He and I rarely complained to each other about anything of a serious nature. Aches and pains were met with either a joke or by stoically ignoring them. That was just the way it was. Even when he was in the hospital himself for a serious operation, we never talked about it while I was visiting. He usually complained because I was wasting valuable fishing time in his hospital room with him instead of being out there on the streams.

When Judy and I got the original diagnosis that the doctors suspected they hadn't removed the whole cancer and that it had probably already spread to other parts of her body, we didn't tell many people. But when I saw Corser, he maneuvered me into a quiet place in church on a Sunday morning and asked for the real story. He knew me too well, so I confessed our fears.

For the first and only time I ever knew him, I saw a tear in his eye. He quickly turned away, surreptitiously wiped his face, and said, "Damn!"

We never spoke of it again. But after that I noticed that whenever he came to pick me up to go off on one of our excursions, he always got out of the truck, came into the house, and talked to Judy for a while. That was out of character for him. Or maybe, now that I think about it, it was totally *in* character. His *real* character.

Judy and I both appreciated it, and our subsequent trips to stay with him in the Adirondacks every year were somehow a bit more poignant. I guess you really don't appreciate anything in life until you come to see that nothing lasts forever.

In an earlier chapter, I called the decade of the '70s "The Great Illusion." I stand by that statement. But I tell these stories about Corser to illustrate an important point. In one sense, all of life is an illusion. Nothing is really as it seems. Even at the biological level of cellular structures, and the general physics level of elementary particles, everything is different from our perception of it. But there are things not made up of cells and particles that are real just the same. You can't dissect them and put them under a microscope. You can't pour them into a test tube. I'm talking about things such as love and respect, friendship and compassion, understanding and shared experience. When you stop to think about it, those are the things that last forever. Even in the midst of illusion they transcend our perceived reality.

My time with Corser was what I remember from the '70s and the next decade to follow. Many have written--and will continue to write—about Vietnam and civil rights. Historians will carefully parse the great changes that took place in Western civilization during that tumultuous time. No one will ever write about Corser and me, but that's the story that will last long after the universe grows cold and eventually passes away into darkness. It's an eternal story. It's real. It transcends the material world.

At his funeral, he had asked me to recite, in his words, "The whole 'home is the hunter' thing. You know the one."

When that time came, and with a great deal of difficulty, I managed to stand in the pulpit and recite the old Robert Louis Stevenson poem he was referring to. It's called *Requiem*:

> *Under the wide and starry sky,*
> *Dig the grave and let me lie.*
> *Glad did I live and gladly die,*
> *And I laid me down with a will.*
>
> *This be the verse you grave for me:*
> *Here he lies where he longed to be;*
> *Home is the sailor, home from the sea,*
> *And the hunter home from the hill.*

It may sound trite to say this, but in Corser's case it is true nonetheless. He is gone but not forgotten.

See you over the next hill, Don, when the New England October skies are beyond blue and the leaves are starting to show off their annual display, before they, too, succumb to their inevitable end. Bring the coffee. And don't forget the doughnuts!

Cosmo and Me

Chapter 4:
Becoming What We Despised
(the 1980s)

THE CULTURE

Kids and responsibilities tame even the most dedicated hippie, to say nothing about fire-breathing preachers. It's easy to enter into a Faustian bargain with the god of economics when you cut your needs to the bone and they go and raise the price of the bone. Besides, others I knew well were reaping huge profits. When do the Just get rewarded?

Every decade is unique and different from every other decade, but to live through the 1980s while navigating your thirties--with the subsequent build-up to mid-life crisis--was to experience a severe test of moral and ethical fiber, to say nothing of spiritual commitment. Imagine a perfect storm designed by an egotistical devil who wants to conquer the world with an agenda of hedonism, and you come pretty close.

Consider the changing technological landscape, for instance. It began with a new video game called Pac-Man that beckoned people to flock to a new invention called the video game. The game, at first only found in arcades, eventually made the jump to home television, and Americans were off to the races. If those of you who are now gamers can't relate to such primitive entertainment, rest assured that not everyone caught the bug right away. Many were too busy trying to solve the mystery of another sensation called the Rubik's Cube. Now, there was a way to spend your spare time!

Think about what happened during just the first year of the decade:

- In February 1980 the U.S. hockey team pulled off the "Miracle on Ice," defeating the Soviet Union in the semifinals of the Olympics held at Lake Placid, New York. The musical soundtrack to the event was provided by Chuck Mangione, who helped make the idea of Jazz Fusion, which had been bubbling around since the late '60s, explode on AM radio. Different styles of rhythm, propelled by such innovative artists as drummer Steve Gadd and bassist Tony Levin, would soon be superseded by mesmerizing mechanical tracks that would find their ultimate expression in a dance phenomenon called Disco in the 1970s. But before the turn to the dark side, there was once real blood in those beats.
- In April, media tycoon Ted Turner decided that people might want to hear news 24 hours a day. The idea was that his new Cable News Network (CNN) would have the time to bring news in depth to the American public. I doubt even he knew at the time that he was unleashing a new, shortened, and superficial concept called the "news cycle." As of this writing, there is no end in sight. In wasn't long before corrupt politicians learned that if they got caught with their proverbial hand in the cookie jar, all they had to do was wait a few minutes and people would soon be drawn to something else.
- Also in April, the US abortive attempt to rescue American hostages, who had been held in Iran since 1979, in effect brought about the downfall of Jimmy Carter and ushered in the reign of Ronald Reagan. It was the beginning of trickle-down economics, burgeoning budgets, the fall of the Berlin Wall, the end of the Cold War, the Iran Contra arms scandal, and the political division between "conservatives" and "liberals" that is still playing out in American history.
- Perhaps Gaia herself decided it was time to issue a few warnings. In May, Mt. St. Helens in Washington state erupted, killing more than 50 people.

- But life continued on. The *Star Wars* franchise ushered in long lines outside theaters when people flocked to see *The Empire Strikes Back*. Those who weren't at the theater stayed home to find out who shot J. R. Ewing in *Dallas*, or alternately laugh and cry at the latest episode of *M*A*S*H*. "Must-See TV" was on the horizon, just a few short years away.
- At the end of 1980, the music died again. John Lennon was murdered by a deranged gunman in New York City.

And that was merely the first year of the decade. We went on to discover something called acquired immunodeficiency syndrome when the Center for Disease Control issued its first report about AIDS.

IBM released its Model 5150 personal computer. Very few of us felt the earth shake at the announcement, but it did. *Time* magazine pictured a computer on its cover, calling it the "Machine of the Year," much to the chagrin of Apple's Steve Jobs, who thought he was a shoo-in that year. Two years later, the Internet was born.

The whole revolution blinded us to another reality. A mobile phone, appropriately called "The Brick," was manufactured and popularized in the movies when Michael Douglas, aka *Wall Street's* Gordon Gekko, was shown making calls from a beach, untethered by land lines. Did anyone guess at the time what was coming?

At long last, it was an important decade for women in the news. Sandra Day O'Connor became the first female justice to sit on the Supreme Court. Dianna Spencer became Princes Dianna during a wedding that was televised live to millions of people around the globe. We watched, of course, never knowing what that kind of exposure can eventually do to a person. Oprah could have warned her, but Winfrey's star was just beginning to rise.

By the middle of the decade, we began to visualize just how far we had been blinded when it came to environmental concerns. Rachael Carson had warned us about a possible *Silent Spring* way back in the '60s, but it took a deadly nuclear power plant accident in Chernobyl and the grounding of the *Exxon Valdez* oil tanker to wake us up to the environmental havoc of which we were capable.

It was a decade for the ages, but when you're negotiating your own personal difficulties, who has time to sit back and reflect? Like many others of my generation, I spent the time struggling just to hold on and make ends meet. Families are expensive, and it didn't help my frame of mind when everyone else seemed to be getting ahead while I was forced to say to my wife, "Honey, I'm going to town. I'd better take *the* dollar."

I had made a deliberate choice to accept poverty as the price I paid for individual freedom. But my poverty now came with a deliberate price tag. I wasn't the only one in the slowly sinking boat anymore. I had a wife and kids to support. My choices affected them. Had I chosen wrong? Was I being selfish? Why should they suffer just so I didn't have to answer to a boss and depressing work environment, to say nothing of having the time to go hunting and fishing with Corser? It's the kind of self-examination that haunts me to this day.

When I ask the question, "Had I chosen wrong?" it's not an idle question. I need to jump ahead here because only much later in life did I come to understand that my choice was probably right. And it was confirmed by a most unexpected person—my dad.

Let's jump ahead a few decades.

If only inanimate objects could talk. What tales they would tell! Like this one, for instance: For many years after my dad retired, a gold clock resided in a place of honor in his living room. It had been awarded to him when he retired from the Amoco Oil Company and dominated any room in which it was placed.

I had assumed that the clock held nothing but good memories of a life well-lived, but one day I learned that it carried, at best, mixed metaphors.

My mother, although certainly loyal to my father, knew the whole story and had let her feelings show from time to time. I didn't always understand her hidden allusions when I was young, but as I grew older they began to penetrate my consciousness. In effect, she prepared me, although I am sure she never realized she was doing it, so that when the time came I would come to understand a part of my father that he very rarely, if ever, revealed to anyone. To do so would bring up a psychological/philosophical conflict that I don't think he ever fully came to terms with. It would have meant turning away from a long-held belief.

Dad was not a deep thinker. He was a wonderful man and had many positive attributes, but I could never get him to engage in conversations that delved too deeply into subjects that have consumed my life—issues of meaning and relevance. I'm sure he had such thoughts, but, perhaps because he was a product of his age, he usually suppressed them. Maybe that's why we could never attain the closeness that I so wanted.

He loved the American Oil Company, the church, and music, probably in that order. As for me, although we shared a love for the last two, I resented the mysterious corporation that had so messed with our family life. We were transferred, on average, every four years. My sister and I hated it. She never really forgave him for it, even though she married a man who was similar, in many respects, to my father. My mother quietly fumed, but went along, as wives back then were expected to do.

(She often told me about the day she had a house full of kids, hosting my fifth birthday party, when dad called from work, telling her she had to pack a bag because he had to fly to Detroit that very night. And, by the way, we would soon be moving. How she managed to finish the birthday party and handle all that, I'll never know. But she resented it to her dying day. She even brought it up during one of the last lucid conversations we ever had.)

My dad and I shared a love for music, but we appreciated it in different ways. I was all about the art and the beauty. He was more into technique and the ability of the performer. We both loved the church, but he was in it primarily for the music and the organization. Once the anthem was finished, he could relax. That's when I thought the service really started.

I think that was why he was probably secretly proud of the career I chose. I use the word "secretly" by design. I was a musician and a pastor, two things he probably had once wanted to be but put aside for financial reasons. To him, such activities were not a "real" job.

But the corporate aspects of both careers never interested me, so I chose small churches and small towns in which to utilize my talents. He often chastised me for not progressing upward. He considered me "partially retired," in his words. To my great regret, I never told him that I had a lifetime aversion to any organization that even came close to resembling what he had chosen for a living.

All this background may seem far afield from a story about a clock, but that clock represents the whole issue. It stood as a powerful reminder of a corporate greed that, only near the end of his life, did dad ever reveal to me. It took that long, and, to be honest, a couple of his superbly mixed Manhattans, for him to finally bring up the whole story.

First, some background.

In 1911 the Supreme Court ruled that the Standard Oil Company, founded by John D. Rockefeller and his business partners, was in violation of the Sherman Antitrust Act. They were said to have created an illegal monopoly and were divided into 34 various geographical areas. This marked the beginning of a long, involved, political fight that is still going on. The company's way of dealing with this was to gradually merge with other, smaller companies, take their name, so as to remove the corporate stigma, and go right on expanding. These successors became the core of today's oil industry.

Standard Oil of New Jersey, for instance, merged with Exxon, and then with Mobile, to become Exxon Mobile in 1999. The Standard Oil Company of Indiana merged with the American Oil Company and became Amoco. Later, Amoco merged with British Petroleum, becoming BP.

This last merger led to my dad retiring and receiving his clock. It happened in this way.

When my dad was young, corporations had begun their take-over of the United States. Eisenhower warned us that the greatest enemy to the American way of life was the military/industrial complex, and he was correct. The oil industry, for instance, has consistently and successfully been opposed to any action on climate control. What we witness today has revealed the worldwide results of their actions. (After dad retired, I called him on the morning of the huge BP oil spill in the Gulf of Mexico. I didn't have to say a thing. As soon as he recognized my voice, before either of had said anything beyond Hello, he said, "I know. You're right!" It turns out he had already heard the news.)

But when dad was young, corporations such as Standard Oil, Ford, and other giants demanded and received loyalty from their employees. People like my father were expected to put the company before everything else, including, much to my mother's disapproval, family. Executives were moved across the country at a moment's notice with little or no thought to the effect this might have on wives relocating and kids changing schools.

Dad had started out as a stock boy, and eventually climbed the ladder of success to regional importance. He and others like him were well paid, of course, and that's why families went along. High salaries, some of which were paid in company stock in order to reduce costs and promote loyalty, were the rule in those days.

Make no mistake, it worked. The reason oil companies and their ilk had such political power was because they employed thousands upon thousands of registered voters whose allegiance was to the company. You were a "Ford Man," a "Standard Oil Man," or a "Railroad Man." Such corporations had provided you with a substantial living, including a house in the suburbs. You owned thousands of dollars of stock, which would provide a handsome retirement, and you were loyal to the core. You sacrificed for your company, and you expected your company to sacrifice for you.

But somehow that all began to change. Corporate greed began to sacrifice even amongst its own employees. People who were high up in the company, such as my father, could see the writing on the wall. Their hope was to hang on until retirement and get out before the whole thing fell apart.

This was the background to the one and only negative conversation dad and I ever had about his career with Amoco.

On the day he talked about it, I had remarked that the clock, which was right in front of us, seemed like a shrine of sorts. I asked him why they gave him a clock rather than the standard gold watch.

I didn't expect his answer: "I guess they were glad to see me go."

I was shocked. "Why?" I asked him. "You were always there when they needed you."

Thus it was that he told me the story of his retirement. He had known that something was going on—something was in the wind. He had heard scuttlebutt about mergers and acquisitions, and in his position as regional accountant manager had noticed suspicious expenditures. He had even been approached and asked if he might be open to a move to Oklahoma. For the first and only time in his career, he said no. Having recently bought some retirement property in Michigan, he had no desire to move to Oklahoma. Although my mother never said anything, I think she might have finally put her foot down.

Things quieted down for a while, but one day my dad's boss--with whom he shared a friendship as well as a business relationship—stuck his head in my dad's office and asked if he had a minute to talk.

When he came in, he closed the door. That wasn't normal.

"Don't you have enough years and seniority to take early retirement?" he asked.

Dad was puzzled.

"Sure," he said, "but my retirement package will be better if I wait a few years."

"Why not go ahead, maybe get a part time job somewhere, and enjoy your years while you're still young enough to play golf and do some fishing?"

To say the least, bells went off. His boss was not permitted to release confidential information, but he could still drop some hints. In dad's words, "Thank God I got the message."

He later learned that the merger with BP was coming, but not yet made public. Amoco was getting its house in order. By refusing to move to Oklahoma, dad had, in effect, defied the company. He was earning too much to keep him on in anything less than a top executive position. And his boss knew it. In short, an excuse would have been found, and dad would have been let go just a few years short of retirement. He had become expendable. All his years of work had come to nothing. Loyalty, it seems, at least when it came to dealing with corporations, was a one-way street.

Dad announced his retirement, was given a party (at which he was awarded a gold clock), got his name in the paper, and landed a part-time job at the Interlochen Arts Academy, right across the lake from where his retirement house was being built. He held that job until his retirement officially kicked in five years later, played a lot of tennis, and did a lot of fishing.

As it turned out, every time he looked at that clock, he was reminded, at least subliminally, of a life that had, at the end, sent some really deeply mixed messages. It represented a good life that he had been able to provide for his family. It also represented corporate greed and expediency, which, for all his life, he had decided to ignore.

It didn't help any when he came to realize, near the end, why I had intuitively chosen to reject the thing he had most believed in. The only clue I ever got that he thought about this at all was when he once came to visit me at what was to be my final church and my final pastorate. He brought his trombone, and he and I played together in church for the last time. After the coffee hour and quite a few complimentary comments from parishioners, he said, in an almost "by-the-way," offhand comment, "Maybe you made the right choice."

If only inanimate objects could talk. In terms of present-day American metaphors, what a tale this clock would tell!

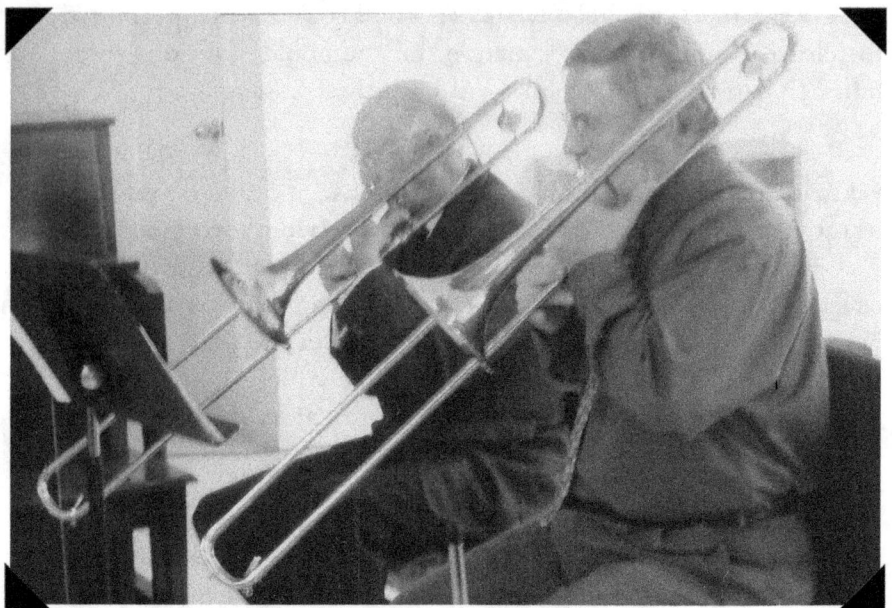

Dad and I played together in church for the last time — Port Orange United Church of Christ, FL (2007).

But I didn't know all this back in the '80s, so I just blundered along.

As it turned out, the decade began badly for me when I was notified of the death of my sister. Just as had been the case when I learned about the suicides of my two mentors, my sister had traveled too far down the road of despair. Eventually, she could see no other way out of the darkness, and she, too, took her own life.

To make matters even worse, the next years were spent caring for my wife, who was slowly dying of cancer. When faced with death, all a person can usually do is just keep on going through the motions of life. Although I spent time wondering if I had made the right choice by staying in a low-paying job, like most decisions in life I've ever made, that one was probably guided. If I had moved to a bigger church, a bigger town, and more responsibility, I would have uprooted my kids and not had the time to transport Judy to hospitals and radiation sessions while she was dealing with the effects of chemotherapy. Once again, I think I was being led, not pushed. But as the decade began, I had no idea what lay ahead.

THE QUESTION

If you gain the whole world, do you really lose your soul?

"Lead us not into temptation, but deliver us from evil."

Those are the familiar words of the prayer attributed to Jesus in the Gospels According to Matthew and Luke. Protestants call it the "Lord's Prayer." In Catholic tradition it is usually referred to as the "Our Father." Most folks who are my age and attended public school in the United States grew up saying these words every morning, right after reciting the Pledge of Allegiance. It all stopped when the U.S. Supreme Court delivered two landmark decisions: *Engel v. Vitale* on June 25, 1962, and *Abington School District v. Schempp* on June 17, 1963. Both declared school-sponsored prayer and Bible readings unconstitutional. When I started teaching college courses on world religions in the 1990s, I would still get the occasional student who would swear that "removing prayer" from public schools brought about the downfall of morality in America, but at the time, I really can't remember anyone who really took such prayer seriously. Back then, it was just something you said. It wasn't necessarily something you believed.

But the words certainly took on special significance for me as the decade of the '80s came to a close and I passed my fortieth birthday. To make financial ends meet in those days, I had to work constantly. After teaching public school music part-time, three days a week, while quite often working 40 more hours at my "part-time" church job, I would usually conduct a choir rehearsal followed by a 90-minute lecture at a Bible study on Monday night, lead a community choir that met on Tuesday night, attend a church meeting on Wednesday night, lead another Bible study on Thursday night, play a dance job from 8:00 to midnight on Friday night, officiate at a Saturday morning wedding, play for a wedding reception from 1:00 to 4:00, grab a quick bite to eat, and then play a jazz gig at night that usually ended between midnight and 1:00. I would get home bleary eyed and fall asleep by 2:00 on Sunday morning and then wake up at 6:00 in time to lead two church services, grab a quick nap, and then drive halfway across the state to sing a gospel concert at a church that might be 50 or 60 miles away. I would usually get home by 11:00 in time to fall into bed, wake up the next day, and start all over again. Besides all this, I was both a cub scout and girl scout leader so that my kids would have a scouting experience, and, in later years, chauffeured them to dance classes and sporting events. I wrote and produced a pre-recorded, daily drive-time radio show and drove my wife to a hospital two hours north for chemotherapy treatments or a different hospital an hour south for radiation treatments, depending on how her cancer was advancing.

For years I would look at my calendar on the first of the month, and if I noticed an evening or two with no meetings, or an occasional weekend with no club dates for my band, I considered it a luxury. Snow storms, especially on weekends, were a gift from God.

Why did I do it? In a word, money. We were constantly running out of paycheck before the bills got paid. In a good year, if I cleared $12,000, I considered myself flush with cash. But when I added up medical bills, food and clothes for a growing family, gasoline (which got really expensive after 1979), and all the rest of our expenses, they were lean years.

They were also the years when I sometimes threw caution to the winds, broke out a new credit card, and began to do silly things such as riding a bicycle across the country, running in triathlons, or disappearing for a few days to hike the Appalachian Trail just to try to stay sane. In those days, before cell phones, no one could reach you if you were out on the road, training for a race or the next long-distance bike ride.

Is it any wonder, then, that, when faced with a real temptation, I almost caved?

It all began after my wife died.

I'm going to leave names and dates out of what follows in order to protect the innocent. Maybe even the guilty. One day I received a package in the mail that contained no return address.

Cosmo and Me

Journey's End: Pacific to Atlantic — Plum Island, MA (1982).

A significant event had occurred in my life just prior to this that involved a very serious medical procedure. Operations for acoustic neuromas are, these days, more common than they were back then. I had put off having myself checked out by a specialist even after I became aware that I seemed to have lost significant hearing in one ear. After spending nine years transporting my wife to doctors while she fought what eventually proved to be a losing battle with cancer, I had put off my own health problems.

When I eventually gave in and made a visit to my doctor, I was told to wait a year and see what happened. That didn't sound right, so I consulted a different doctor and got a second opinion. He immediately booked a CAT scan. When the results came in, he sent me to a hospital two hours north, the same hospital I had visited so often with my wife. It was the nearest facility in those days that could do MRIs.

The results were shocking. I had a tumor growing near my brain stem.

When they first found it, it was the size of a pea. After removal a month later, it had grown to the size of a grape. If I had hesitated even a few months, I could have died. As it was, I lost the hearing in my right ear. But I considered myself lucky. Before the operation took place, I was told that three things could happen, and all of them were bad:

- I might not make it through the operation. They were going to cut a hole in my skull, take out the tumor, and then replace the piece of bone they had removed. The operation required two doctors working on me for about nine or ten hours. Working that close to my brain stem was tricky. Anything could happen and they wanted me to have my affairs in order. That involved making arrangements for my two kids, who had just lost their mother to cancer.

- The tumor might have already compromised the nerves on the right side of my face. I could experience something that looked like a stroke, which would have involved sagging in my right eye, the right corner of my mouth, and the right side of my face. Everything I did to earn money involved either talking, singing, or playing the trombone. This result would definitely have eliminated all of the above.

- I would most probably lose the hearing in my right ear. For a musician, this was bad enough. But at least I could live with it.

As it turns out, fate chose door number 3, but for a period of about two weeks after the procedure I flirted with the second option. It scared the living daylights out of me.

I also came home from the hospital while addicted to morphine. They called it "pain medication." I didn't know. All I knew was that something was happening to me that made my skin crawl and kept me up pacing the floors all night long, unable to sit still. It was terrible, made worse by that fact that they didn't tell me what the problem was until I had pretty much kicked it on my own, by accident, as it were. I had no experience with such things and didn't know what was going on.

Two weeks later, when the doctor told me, long-distance over the phone, that I had been going through narcotic withdrawal, I was incensed. I insisted I had never used drugs in my life. Then he told me that my "pain medication" had been morphine. To put it mildly, I was upset.

But what made the whole experience even worse was something that was probably quite petty. For the last few decades, whenever any member of my congregation had been sick in the hospital, I had visited them. I considered it really important that folks shouldn't have to go through a crisis alone. Rain or shine, busy or not, night or day, I had been there for them.

But I was in the hospital for two weeks, and no one had come to visit me. Not one person. Ever. Granted, the hospital was a two-hour drive from my home, but, still....

So, was I a little bitter when I received that package in the mail, the one that contained no return address?

I was. And more than a little. On top of all that, my income had really dropped during the last few months. Expenses had piled up, and I didn't see much hope for a change anytime soon.

When I opened the plain, manila envelope, I thought I was the victim of somebody's idea of a joke. It contained only an old magazine, with no cover. I opened it up while sitting at my kitchen table and was, truth be told, pretty bewildered. It was some kind of travel magazine, but it was at least a few months old, and the cover had been torn off.

I was about to throw it away when something fluttered out and landed on the table. It was a hundred-dollar bill. Leafing through the magazine, I discovered another one. Then another. Carefully examining each page, I found ten of them. I was staring at a thousand dollars with a mystified expression on my face, having no idea who had sent it to me. The envelope was postmarked from Las Vegas, Nevada. I knew no one who lived even close to Nevada, let alone Las Vegas.

For about two weeks I could only wonder what this was about. Then, late one night, I received a phone call from a very distant relative of a friend.

He asked a simple question: "Did you get my present?"

"Was that from you?" I didn't even remember his name. I had just heard about him being out west somewhere.

"There's more where that came from, if you can use it. I'll be in Massachusetts next week. Can I come visit?"

Being naïve is sometimes an asset, but sometimes it isn't. I thought he might have a job offer for me. As it turned out, he did. When he came to dinner the next week we tried to hem and haw and talk about things we had in common. But that didn't last long. We didn't *have* anything in common.

He was very well off, that was apparent. And I soon found out how he made his money. He was a drug dealer. He was also looking for someone who would carry drugs up from Mexico for him. He explained how a minister who had recently lost his wife might want to take an all-expenses-paid vacation at a Mexican tourist spot. It would seem perfectly natural. There, I would be contacted and given a package to bring back home. I would be carefully instructed how to do this so as not to attract attention at the border. A measure of naïveté would come in handy when dealing with border guards. Then, after arriving home, I would be contacted again. I would deliver the package, unopened of course, and be given a sum of money. No exact figure was mentioned, but it would be a lot of money.

Ministers are seldom speechless, but I was. I had no idea what to say. I think I remained that way for about a minute and a half before I turned him down. But what bothers me to this very day is that for a minute and a half I wasn't thinking about ethics or morality. I never asked myself, "What would Jesus do?"

No, I worried about two things:

First, I worried about getting caught.

Second, I worried that if I wasn't caught, and made a lot of money, it would be very easy to do it again.

A few months ago, Barbara, my wife of 20 years now, and I watched Clint Eastwood's movie *The Mule* in which an ornery old horticulturalist becomes a delivery driver for a Mexican drug cartel, driven to his decision because of dire financial straits. To say the least, it brought on cold sweats and a few sleepless nights. For the first time, I told Barb about my experience of long ago. To my surprise, she had a similar story to tell. She was, at the time, a single mom, living on St. Croix in the Caribbean, with a young child. Perfect cover. She, too, was faced with the same temptation, and offered similar inducements. She, too, had turned down the offer, and for the same reasons.

For the first time I realized my experience was not unique. How many people have been approached with a similar temptation? How many had refused? How many had succumbed?

I'm glad I chose wisely and not given in because of bitterness toward life and financial problems, but, to this day, I wish I had made my decision based on an inherent morality rather than the fear of getting caught. I often play the "What If?" game. How would my life have turned out had I chosen differently?

I share this story because I have come to believe that, beginning in the 1980s, American culture faced a similar choice. It was a time of financial prosperity during which we became the envy of the world. Young people, especially, who understood high tech and were comfortable with what the newfound wild, wild West of Internet "dot-coms" could accomplish, grabbed for the brass ring and became unbelievably wealthy. Some of them are now among the richest men in the world.

But when you are faced with great power and wealth, having not yet achieved a solid base of morality and spiritual dimension, is it possible to gain the whole world but lose your soul in the process? Is that what happened to the America I once knew? Did we reach too high, too fast, and surpass our ethical development in the process?

How else can we explain the fact that the wealth gap between rich and poor grew so fast? How else do we explain the loss of what in the '50s and '60s was called the middle class? During those halcyon days, when CEOs made about 11% more than their workers, one good, solid, middle-class wage could buy a house and car, provide food for the table, and even send kids to college.

These days it takes at least two incomes—and often even that isn't enough—while CEOs bring home hundreds, even thousands of times what their workers earn.

I'm not a trained economist. I can't speak with any authority when it comes to explaining the ins and outs of supply-side economics or the supposed virtue of a trickle-down economy. But it felt to me as though something broke in the '80s. Maybe it had as much to do with my own personal life situation as a national crisis. Perhaps it was even a little of both. But on more than one occasion I have since had conversations with people whom I respect in which we asked a pertinent question: Has America gained the whole world, but lost its soul?

If so, the '80s are a good place to look in order to find the moment the fracture started becoming obvious. It took longer than one decade, of course. The process started earlier than that and is still going on, but if you want to find a good metaphor those years offer some chilling examples.

I have a favorite poem that I have quoted in other books. It was written by James Russell Lowell. Here is a portion of it:

> *Once to every man and nation, comes the moment to decide,*
> *In the strife of truth with falsehood, for the good or evil side ...*
> *Though the cause of evil prosper, yet the truth alone is strong;*
> *Though her portion be the scaffold, and upon the throne be wrong;*
> *Yet that scaffold sways the future, and behind the dim unknown,*
> *Standeth God within the shadow, keeping watch above His own.*

I wonder sometimes if those words are more prophetic than metaphorical. Has America made her choice, or does the choice still remain in the future? Is it really one choice, or does it continually offer itself? And if the latter is the case, is there a proverbial straw that breaks the camel's back? Is it possible to go so far down the wrong road that we get lost and are not able to find our way back? Is there a reason cultures fail and collapse, only to be covered over by the dust of history? And if the choice presents itself, are we sometimes not able to see it as such until it's too late?

If the answer to any of these questions is yes, we can, hopefully, take comfort in the last words of Lowell's poem:

> *... Behind the dim unknown,*
> *Standeth God within the shadow, keeping watch above His own.*

Noble words, to be sure. But are they true? Is there really a God who is looking down upon us, as I professed to believe so fervently at that time of my life? While America was groping its way forward toward the spiritual crisis that lay before it, I faced my own dark time of the soul during that pivotal decade. My own spiritual crisis was at hand. It wasn't just the decision to choose whether or not to become a criminal in the eyes of the law. It involved something even more serious.

I've shared this story in print before, but I need to include it here because it quite literally changed the course of my life.

For years I had called myself a Christian fundamentalist, although "Evangelical" was probably closer to the truth. You have to understand something about fundamentalists, whether their ideologies are religious, political, social, or philosophical in nature. Whenever you meet someone who claims to know THE TRUTH, you can safely assume two things:

First of all, they don't.

Second, they're probably obnoxious.

All religions breed right-wing fundamentalists. Political parties and scientific communities do it, too. Someone gets to be an expert, gathers a following, and then, suddenly, a fundamentalist is born. This is the person who knows it all, at least as far as "it" pertains to his or her own body of knowledge. They determine the fundamentals, the things you simply have to believe, if you are going to be in their group. Those who accept the fundamentals are "sound." They can be trusted. They teach their system to others, who probably do not completely understand everything. But they believe in the leader, so they go along.

During the 1980s, I had such a following. I had a radio show, was speaking at various churches and civic groups about different religious topics, and believed that the earth was only 6,000 years old. I could support that belief with many different Scripture verses and could be very obnoxious at parties and social gatherings.

I now freely confess that I thought I knew most of the answers. I was a Christian fundamentalist, through and through. I bought and taught the whole party line. Although I am no longer a fundamentalist, I still call myself a Christian, even though I'm sure many of my former Christian friends and acquaintances would question that label as it applies to me these days. For a while, in the middle part of the decade, I walked a pretty tight rope and even came within a hair's breadth of falling off.

Here's what happened.

My Christian label back then was New England Congregationalist. We were descended from good Puritan stock. Perhaps "stocks" would be a better name, given the puritanical penchant for punishing protagonist perpetrators. (Somebody once described a Puritan as someone who suffered from the fear that somewhere in the world someone might be happy.)

Things have changed somewhat since Puritan times. As a matter of fact, the United Church of Christ, my denomination, is descended in part from Puritan roots but has the reputation of being very liberal. Back then, though, I wasn't. The more I studied my Bible and built my intellectual systematic theology on what I considered to be its inerrant texts, the more I came to believe that I was preaching THE TRUTH!

It made perfect sense to me, then, that the church down the street, since they didn't agree with me, wasn't preaching the truth. Since my way was God's way—after all, it came straight from the Bible—then they must be wrong. If they were wrong, they must be deceived. If they were deceived, they must not be of God.

See how it works?

Okay, it probably sounds silly to you. Maybe even dangerous. But I'll bet you have some of your own ideas, either religious or political, wherein you feel like a true believer while knowing in your heart of hearts that your Uncle Fred is dead wrong. (By the way, the older we get, the harder it is to avoid this trap.)

Fundamentalists are not very tolerant. "Those who are not with us are against us!" That kind of thing. For a time just prior to 2020, even the president said it. It's pretty common.

What made this whole philosophical structure fall apart was the fact that one day I risked being open enough to consider what was--to me, at least—a heretical idea as I sat at my desk putting together a sermon about a topic I have long since forgotten, although I do remember that it seemed very important at the time. Following my usual M.O., I was compiling biblical proof texts right and left, selecting from here and there and arranging them in some kind of order, while imagining myself bludgeoning an audience to death with incontrovertible evidence.

A nagging thought kept pestering me, one that I had dimly noticed for some time but had successfully managed to keep safely at bay. It had been crouching in the shrubbery of my mind, like a hungry lion waiting to pounce. Finally, it did.

You see, I had for many years been studying the Bible in more depth than most people ever bother to do. I knew it backwards and forwards. I knew how Romans related to Genesis and Revelation related to Isaiah. I saw it as one long story. But the very fact of my familiarity became the problem. When it came to content, the Bible held no secrets from me. We were like an old married couple who knew each other's strengths and weaknesses, so I was very much aware that it contained troubling references that seemed contradictory, inaccurate, or downright wrong. I had learned how to skirt around those portions, pretending they didn't exist. I had become similar to a lawyer, arguing in defense of a client I secretly knew was guilty. When I finally opened myself up to admitting it, there in the privacy of my quiet office, it led to my downfall.

Put simply, the bottom line was this. Over the years I had come to base my entire theology on biblical proof texts. Most funda-mentalists and evangelicals do. But what if it could be demon-strated to my satisfaction that the Bible was not without what I would call error? What if that wonderful collection of wisdom and inspiration even contained some discrepancies or historical inaccuracies? Worse yet, what if the original authors never intended their work to be considered inerrant? In other words, what if the modern doctrine of inerrancy was something I was superimposing on documents meant to be understood in quite a different way?

Do you see the problem? If an argument about the existence of God hinges on proof texts selected from a Bible that is said to be without error, then all someone has to do is show that the Bible contains some discrepancies, and the argument is over. God simply ceases to exist.

In other words, I wasn't preaching about God anymore. I was preaching about an inerrant, infallible Bible. In my theology, the Bible had taken the place of God.

Clearly, I had a problem. My whole faith system was shaken to the core. Everything I believed was suddenly called into question. All the stuff I had studied in seminary about historical criticism of the Bible came back to haunt me. I couldn't ignore it anymore.

At that moment, I decided I would have to leave the ministry and stick to teaching music. I was completely devastated. I no longer had anything to say from the pulpit.

Right then I decided to go on retreat for a few days. I had built a small log cabin up in New Hampshire, so I decided to go up there for a while, be alone, and see if I could find some kind of answer.

While I was there, I encountered another opportunity for openness.

Three days into my lonely retreat I hiked up a mountain that I had climbed a dozen times before. It exactly suited my needs that day because it was high enough to be a challenge but, when you got to the top, opened up to a magnificent view of miles and miles of countryside. Most important—I had never seen anybody else up there.

Today was different. Topping the last rise, discouraged and completely at odds with myself, lost in the terribly despondent throes of a real mid-life crisis of the soul, I came out of the trees and met, face to face, so to speak, a nude woman sunbathing on a rock.

Nothing in the world is more threatening to a true-blue fundamentalist preacher than a nude woman on a rock, surrounded by nature. Isis unbound! At first glance she represented everything that was foreign to my way of thinking. She looked primitive, pagan, sinful, and worst of all, absolutely free.

Fundamentalists have an unhealthy fear of too much freedom.

I turned to walk away, averting my eyes from such unbridled sinfulness as a naked human body. But before I could take more than a step or two, she yelled, "Hi! Come on over and join me."

What could I do? I mean, I was up there in front of God and everybody, fearfully certain that my entire congregation was going to momentarily step out of the woods in condemnation, and this woman, rather than covering up, was inviting me to join her.

Now, how do you say no to a nude woman on a rock? Every instinct, every one, said, "Get out of here! You remember what happened to Joseph in the book of Genesis. This is definitely, most definitely, the work of the devil. Flee for your life!"

But somehow, I found myself sitting down and talking to her. We talked about everything from reincarnation to crystals, from meditation to ESP. She was interested, really interested, in what I believed and why I believed it. I was fascinated by what she had to say. I had, until then, been utterly opposed to those I called worldly people. But here I was, sitting right next to a living, breathing, nude, worldly person, who wanted to learn more about spiritual formation.

Know what? So did I. Sometime during that long afternoon I realized I was having the first really spiritual conversation I had had in a long time. A philosophical vista opened before me. Here we were—two seekers on different paths—each looking for the same thing—sharing our insights on the journey—helping a fellow traveler along the way.

To this day, I believe that God, whoever He/She/It may be, has a tremendous sense of humor. I can't think of a better way to knock a fundamentalist over the head than by taking him up a mountain, just like Moses, and then, instead of giving him the Ten Commandments, introducing him to a nude woman on a rock. Perhaps James Russell Lowell was right, and God does stand in the shadows, "Keeping watch above His own."

There was absolutely nothing sexual about the meeting. (Well, maybe a little at first—but only for a moment, and only in my mind. I may have been a fundamentalist, but I wasn't dead.) It was a meeting of souls, not bodies. But at the end of our time, when we both went our separate ways, I said to her, "You know, I don't even know your name."

"Does it matter?" she asked, and we both laughed. It didn't matter. What mattered was that we met when we needed to meet, and left the mountain changed. I didn't give up anything that day. I found something. I am still a Christian, but a different kind. My religion has more than enough mystery for me to understand, or even explore sufficiently, in my lifetime. I don't need to window-shop and dabble here and there, although since that day I've done plenty of both. But now I like to talk to people from other traditions, people who can teach me something. I'm not nearly so quick to judge. We are, all of us, in the words of my tradition, children of God.

When I walked down off that mountain, I didn't realize it fully at the time, but I was on a new path. My old life was over. It was time to start building something new. It would take time. All building projects do. But the groundwork was laid. Now it was just a matter of gathering the materials and starting to assemble them. A decade that had begun in turmoil was ending in a quest. Little did I realize that before the quest had barely begun, I would have to do what I had never wanted to do: go mainstream.

Shamanic traditions often recognize threshold guardians. They stand at the point of contact between the world of nature and the spirit. Some American Indian traditions required a vision quest of young men on the threshold of manhood. After fasting and praying for as much as four days, the initiates would often encounter an animal totem that would be their guide for life. Although that did, indeed, happen to me later, I have no doubt that the woman I met on that mountaintop was a real, flesh-and-blood, human being. But she was also a guide who opened the door to a new reality. Was it a coincidence that I met her after three days of solitude? Were those days my period of preparation?

However it happened, that day a left-brained clergyman began his journey to become a right-brained mystic. The path would be long and arduous, full of unexpected twists and turns. In the midst of my frustration and feelings of failure, when it came to turning people's minds toward the world of the spirit, I would find myself just as guilty as those I thought to inspire. I had been searching in my books and my studies, when all the time the answer lay right outside my window. Or perhaps in my heart. It was time to grow up. But, as I came to realize, that's hard to do.

Cosmo and Me

Chapter 5:
Growing Up and Growing Old
(the 1990s)

THE CULTURE

We finally start reading the obituaries. Our sports heroes are now kids! The myth of mid-life crisis becomes reality, and it's not a pretty sight.

Throughout this book I've divided history into ten-year segments. I talked about the '50s, the '60s, the '70s, and the '80s as if somehow events shape themselves conveniently into individual, neatly wrapped, decade-long, packages for our edification. Of course, it doesn't work that way, and we all know it. Life is messy. Our attempts to categorize in order to make some sense of it all is ultimately futile. But the process has something positive going for it. It does promote a systematic understanding that can be helpful.

That aside, we need to remind ourselves that most often events take time to unfold. Something that happens early in life can wait for decades before its ramifications are understood. After all, that's what psychotherapy is usually all about. We look to the past to understand the present. Something happened back then, we repressed it, and it's only now making itself apparent. Realizing it is supposed to bring about freedom and healing.

In my experience, the '90s were all about revealing exactly that kind of process. Of course, I reached life's half-way point as the

Triathlete — Final Triathlon at Daytona Beach, FL (2006).

'90s began to unfold, so I may be prejudiced. Mid-life is a time of retrospection. You are now old enough to know that your life is half over. You still have a lot of time left, God willing, but having already lived more than forty years and seen the first half fly by, you realize you can, for the first time, conceptualize the amount of time remaining. It causes you to assess things in a new way. Gone are any youthful fantasies of living forever. That train has now left the station.

Sometimes you play the "one more time" game. You want to experience a high-point one more time while you're still young enough or have the strength to enjoy it. Stories abound about middle aged men going off with a motorcycle, a hot car, or a younger woman in a futile attempt to relive their youth. In my case, it meant getting in better shape so I could do more long-distance bike trips. It meant participating in more triathlons. It meant becoming the full-time pastor of a bigger church that paid more money. It meant, ugh, identifying with the establishment. I even started to wear a pulpit robe when I preached after I went back to school to finally earn my master's degree. The robe was a uniform, and I embraced it.

But it wasn't just me who was changing. The whole country had changed as well. Take just one area of interest—America's eating habits. We became a nation of fast-food addicts, and our weight and girth changed accordingly. From Eggo waffles to Hot Pockets, the days of a home-cooked meal while the family sat around the dining table were long gone.

Stick with me here. This isn't a sudden course correction. It really fits in with the subject of change. We are what we eat, so if we want to understand why we are the way we are—somewhat bloated in both body and mind--it helps to consider, among many other reasons, of course, what happened to our changing diet. The change happened slowly and had its roots way back in the '50s, but by the '90s

The robe was a uniform, and I embraced it — Easter Sunrise Service at Port Orange, FL (2007).

its effects had become obvious. It's a fascinating study that helps describe what happened to us as a culture.

I started thinking about all this because I was part of the back-to-the-land movement of the '70s and '80s. Many folks my age started to grow bigger and bigger gardens and raise animals for home consumption. We lived on mini-farms, even in cities if zoning permitted it. I didn't live in a city but on a rather small parcel of land on which I found a way to grow all our vegetables, cut wood for heat, and raise three pigs, a passel of rabbits, chickens, a steer, and a lamb every year. For the first time ever, I enjoyed eating things such as tomatoes and brussels sprouts, lamb stew, and chicken dishes for which the recipe didn't begin with "fill the frying pan with oil." Fresh peas and parsnips after a hard frost were a revelation. Homegrown bacon tasted like a new food group.

I had to laugh one particular spring morning at the post office, where the town gathered to share gossip and the latest status report on the state of the black flies. We used to stand in small groups, waving our arms in front of our faces to ward off the day's gathering hoards of the pesky critters. We called it the "Royalston

A New England garden — Roy-alston. MA (late-1970s).

Salute," and anyone who lived there learned it rather quickly. At any rate, one fellow back-to-the-lander, a recent acolyte from New York City, of all places, had recently experienced the wonder of his former chicks all grown up and laying eggs every morning like real, live hens. He was getting a dozen a day. "That's maximum production!" he exclaimed. Clearly you can take the boy out of the city, but you can't take the city's vernacular out of the boy.

I really shouldn't have found it funny. We all ordered chicks through the mail from Sears. It was a common occurrence to find two or even three batches of cheeping, newly hatched chickens being watched over with loving care by the postmistress of our town. The first time I received mine, I, only half tongue-in-cheek, asked her, "Now what do I do with them?"

"You put them in the kitchen behind the wood stove where they'll keep warm."

"How long do I keep them there?"

"Until your wife says, 'Get those chickens out of my kitchen!'"

While a few, like me, grew their own food, the rest of America started ordering out. We have yet to change that trend. American weight climbed like never before.

Bill Glass once played defensive end for the Detroit Lions football team. He was a member of the Fellowship of Christian Athletes and, when I was a young boy, came to our church to speak at a father/son banquet one night. His talk was inspirational and fun, but in the course of regaling us with football stories, he talked about some of the offensive linemen he had to block every Sunday afternoon. Some of them weighed up to 210 pounds! We were impressed. Of course, now, 60 years later, there are many professional football players that top the scales at 300 pounds or more. But back then, a 210-pound-man was gigantic. Because I weigh more than that now, I think of his speech whenever I fly in an airplane that seems to have seats much too small for comfort.

Aside from the return-to-nature experiment that quickly melted before the economic realities of the time, the '90s were a strange decade. On the one hand, it was a fairly happy time as long as you had a decent job and could feed your family.

If you had any money at all, you could invest it in ways that made more money. A five percent return on even simple investments, such as certificates of deposit, was fairly common. There was also a looming thing called the Internet on the horizon that seemed as if it might produce a few laughs before it faded. If you knew how to do it, you could find such things as weather maps that updated themselves every five or six hours. It was fun.

Everyone knew the theme song from *Friends* and watched *Seinfeld* (not that there was anything wrong with that!), so there was a sense of community. Fast food was all the rage. Dance movies were born, at least for those who had never heard of Fred Astaire and Ginger Rogers. The Hubble Space Telescope launched. The Gulf War raged, but we were winning, so that was okay. The median household income grew by ten percent and the Dow Jones by 309 percent. Plus, for the first time in a long, long time, men could go to work without necessarily having to wear neckties. The *New York Times* has since called it America's happiest decade.

Looking back, however, there was also a hollowness to the decade. Something was missing. To be fair, at the time I thought it was just me. But now that I read reports of those times, and talk to others who lived through them, I'm convinced it was more than just my own personal experience. We all seemed to be waiting for something.

Maybe it was the coming turn of the century. What would happen to computers? Would the electric grid shut down? Were Nostradamus and the Mayans right? Would the world as we knew it come to an end? I really didn't know. I certainly hadn't built a fall-out shelter in my backyard. I suspected that nothing drastic would happen. But there was change in the air, and there was nothing anyone could do except wait.

As for me, I felt the need to somehow prepare for a future I didn't yet understand, so I went back to seminary.

There's something freeing about taking courses and realizing you have more experience in ministry than most of your professors. In some cases, I even *knew* more than they did. Their knowledge was specific. Mine was much broader and usually a lot more practical. In some cases, that kind of perspective represents a greater grasp of the subject.

So they couldn't get away with anything. Rarely could they talk about a subject I was not already familiar with, and they soon

After only 20 years!

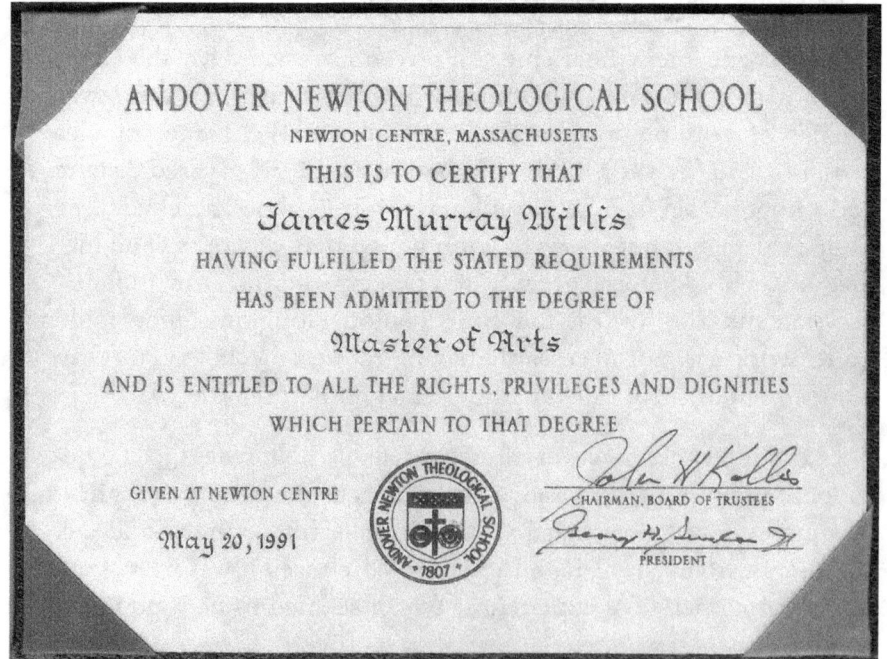

ANDOVER NEWTON THEOLOGICAL SCHOOL

NEWTON CENTRE, MASSACHUSETTS

THIS IS TO CERTIFY THAT

James Murray Willis

HAVING FULFILLED THE STATED REQUIREMENTS

HAS BEEN ADMITTED TO THE DEGREE OF

Master of Arts

AND IS ENTITLED TO ALL THE RIGHTS, PRIVILEGES AND DIGNITIES

WHICH PERTAIN TO THAT DEGREE

GIVEN AT NEWTON CENTRE

May 20, 1991

CHAIRMAN, BOARD OF TRUSTEES

PRESIDENT

learned they couldn't bluff their way through an answer. For the first time in my life, I started to feel comfortable in a classroom, and I actually excelled as a student. I knew what I didn't know, and wanted to correct my shortcomings in subjects I was sure would come in handy. It was liberating in every way and no doubt changed my life. In short, I began to believe in myself.

A few years after I got my new degree, I became a college professor.

THE QUESTION

How do you wisely use the time you have left to complete your quest? And is it worth it?

When you begin what is essentially a new career, things change. When that change happens in mid-life or later, you have already accumulated enough varied experience so that seemingly unrelated areas of life now begin to overlap. New college professors have to learn how to stand in front of a group and lecture, for instance. I had been doing that as a minister for years. New professors must learn how to prepare talking points and then discard them at a moment's notice when your reading of the room reveals they are inadequate for that particular group at that particular time. I was well trained in that skill. New professors need to understand how to take criticism without being personally insulted. That is almost a textbook description of a church pastor.

In short, I took to teaching likes a duck takes to water. And because I was an adjunct professor rather than a tenured full-timer, I didn't have to attend board meetings. I loved it. And the enthusiasm of my students was infectious. No one studies Comparative Religion unless they want to. It's not a required course, so I got the cream of the crop. And my salary didn't depend upon pleasing people. Unlike parishioners, my audience had to come back, whether they agreed with what I said or not. They were engaged. They were inquisitive. They were prepared, for the most part, and I really enjoyed working with them.

My greatest delight was when we paused for a coffee break or lunch, and 18-year-old students right out of high school sat down at a table with 80-year-old auditors who were there just because they wanted to learn more. Two groups from totally different generations were united and engaged over a topic that fascinated them both.

Because I wasn't completely happy with any textbooks I could find, I prepared a glossary of terms we used in class. Little did I know that word list would eventually turn into *The Religion Book: Places, Prophets, Saints, and Seers*, my first published book for Visible Ink Press. That was the book that really began my writing career.

While I was enjoying myself, however, and Americans, as long as they were lucky, were basking in the best of times, things were changing. Too much ease and comfort doesn't prepare a person or a nation for difficult times. Forces were at work that would begin to overpower us a decade later.

The Internet, for instance, was a novelty for many people. Hackers were few and far between, and rather innocuous for the most part. There was as yet no social media to speak of. The hope was that when, or if, it arrived, it would bring people closer together. Theoretically, smart phones came out in 1992, but you could still find a phone booth if you needed one. By 2011, Superman would have been hard-pressed to find a place to change. The term cyberwarfare had not yet entered the lexicon of any but the most far-seeing techies.

The 1990s were, in my opinion, rather like a duck. They looked smooth and serene on the surface, but there was a lot bubbling away below the waterline. We should have seen it coming. Prozac did what very few prescription drugs do. It became trendy. That was a sure sign of something going on.

Now that I look back with clarity, the decisions I had made about my new life were largely terrible. From my youth until way into my twenties and thirties, I had instinctively known that I resented structure and authority. I had hated the regimen of public school. I had, I think wisely, traded the security of big money for

A full-time pastor with office hours, a secretary/office manager, a staff, and all the headaches, board meetings, and responsibilities that went with it. — Port Orange, Fl (2008)

the freedom of part-time work and being my own boss as much as possible. Now I abandoned that plan. I took a job as a full-time pastor with office hours, a secretary/office manager, a staff, and all the headaches, board meetings, and responsibilities that went with it.

Why? The answer was money and recognition. Isn't it always?

After two years, I was miserable, but I wouldn't admit it even to myself. It wasn't just the fact that I now had a full-time job. There were other forces at work—other midlife issues. But when dark thoughts arose, I always managed to convince myself that things would soon improve as soon as I solved this or that problem. Somehow, however, others always arose.

The denomination I served required refresher courses every few years. They were held at a Cape Cod retreat facility. Part of the curriculum included general assessment psychological evaluations conducted by a specialist. When the results were tabulated, I was asked to see the man who administered the test. He sat me down in his office and expressed real concern over my scores. It appeared that I was stressed out and ready for some kind of crisis. He advised me to take it easy and seek some help.

I thought about it all the way home but didn't do anything differently. Summer was coming, and I had a month off. I figured that would help.

Maybe it did, but when the month was over, I almost cried on my way back to work. A few months later, I had a mild heart attack. Luckily, I was driving home from work and was only a few blocks from a hospital when it happened. I managed to pull into the parking lot, and some nurses who were outside on a cigarette break saw right away that I was in trouble. They got a gurney, rushed me into the emergency room, and I pulled through. But I stayed on the job at that church for another year before I realized I just couldn't take it anymore.

It had been five long years, and I should have seen what was happening to me, but I was so ashamed by what I considered my weakness that I couldn't bring myself to do anything about it.

When I finally did, I retreated back to my old life. A part-time church job, a few college courses to teach, some part-time carpentry, and a few jazz gigs on the weekend paid the bills. Not all of them, but most of them. Enough to get by.

A few jazz gigs on the weekend — Canandaigua, NY (1968).

The kind of life we have created for ourselves, the one I had briefly entered, seems like it's the only life possible. And for the most part, it's so entrenched in us that it is that we can't imagine anything else.

I've written about this before in other books, but it's so important that it bears repeating. Our species did not originate and evolve to live the life most of us live these days. We were never meant to be forced to sit in straight rows in school and regurgitate information that poses as an education. We were not meant to give up the prime years of our life serving at the beck and call of authorities who dictate our every movement and determine our fate based on *their* wants and needs. We were not meant to be confined within a cultural system of "going to work" for a certain number of hours every day and a certain number of days every week. But that is just what has happened.

A group of experts who were studying the life of the average American Plains Indian once determined that the Sioux, for instance, were able to supply their needs--during good times, at least--by working for about four hours every day. The rest was spent in community endeavors involving talking, sharing stories, resting, and general relaxation. I have no idea if that survey is substantiated or not, but it sounds so enticing that I've never checked it out. If it's not true, I don't want to know. I just choose to believe it. It gives me justification for feeling the way I do.

For thousands upon thousands of years, we measured time by the season. Eventually we moved to measuring it by the phases of the moon. Then those periods were divided into weeks and days. Finally, the days, which only had three times to remember—morning, noon and night—were divided into hours, and then minutes. Now we're into nanoseconds.

Think how pervasive the whole system is. We get used to time before we go to school. TV programs are half an hour long with commercials every few minutes. Then we go to school and have to be there by a set time or we are punished.

When we go to work, we punch in at a time clock (at least in the old days of a few years ago) and work at a job that pays us to produce so many pieces of work at exactly a predicted amount of time. We check out when the whistle blows at the same time every day, having worked exactly a predetermined number of hours.

We have times to get up, times to eat, times to watch television, and times to go to bed. And then, when we finally retire from the rat race of time, what do they give us? A watch!

The system is so pervasive that it might seem abnormal to state it so succinctly, but given the number of millennia human beings have been on Earth, the whole way of life most of us take for granted is not normal. It is a relatively new phenomenon—an artificial paradigm imposed on us by the authorities who benefit from it. They gain money and power by ensuring that each and every one of us is shaped from a very early age into a specific peg designed to fit into one of their carefully designed holes.

Think about one of the first questions we ask children when they are just beginning the process of maturing into carefully crafted adults: "What do you want to be when you grow up?"

For at least the first 200,000 years of human existence on planet Earth, that question was never, ever asked. What it really means is this: "What set of skills will you develop in order to ensure that an unseen, often unknown, employer can profit off your life before you get too old to supply his needs anymore?"

The retirement age of 65 was set because folks in control of government and commerce needed to throw a sop to those who contributed to their wealth. They thought folks might be grateful to have a few "golden years" on their own before dying at the then-predicted age of 70 for men and 76 for women.

Those who object and try to buck this tightly controlled system are ostracized.

There are still those who try to defy the system. Labor unions, civil rights organizations, entrepreneurs, and support groups are just a few defiant groups that have been tried over the years. Usually, however, those kinds of movements simply try to reform the system or teach how to survive in it rather than question the very basis of its existence. An ancient, hunter/gatherer ancestor who lived 12,000 years ago—just before the beginning of our current civilization—would never have understood the concept of working for someone else's gain unless it was done voluntarily.

Nevertheless, that is the system that enslaves us now. We either play by its rules or pay a great price.

I was now paying the price.

From the standpoint of time, I'm now more than ever convinced of all this. As I write these words, we are in the midst of the third wave of a global pandemic. Americans who were sustained by government checks after being forced to leave their jobs are now able to get back to work. But more than ever they are choosing to be a bit picky when it comes to returning to their former dead-end jobs. They have seen in vivid detail what it took me years to notice. Something is wrong with the social system in which we have recently evolved, but what can replace it?

Back then, I felt the problem but could not find words to adequately understand it let alone express it. That would take years. But now I believe that what was going on in my personal life was also true on a national level. I was sensing deep, intrinsic problems that were percolating under the surface but had not yet burst forth into the light of day. The nation as a whole was doing the same thing.

And so it was that we limped together into the 21st century.

Chapter 6:
Turning the Corner
(Y2K and the Coming of Age)

THE CULTURE

The stew had been brewing since the end of WWII. Economics, politics, inequality, all the "isms" of our day, technology, and mythology floated to the top of a slowly bubbling cauldron. Conspiracy theories ran amok. This leads to the darkest question of all—the one that has been lurking in the wings and sulking behind the curtain ever since we came of age....

On January 1, the annual New Year's Eve rolling parties in America begin. They generally follow the same pattern: The ball drops in New York City and the festivities begin to spread, first to the Midwest, then to the mountains, and finally to the West Coast. People count down the seconds, cheer when they hit zero, kiss their partners, and sing "Auld Lang Syne" at midnight while the band plays on.

But in 2000 there was an added ritual. People waited, sometimes with great apprehension, to see whether the lights would go out as the world plunged into the blackness of a new dark age. In their infancy, computers didn't have a whole lot of storage space—at least by today's standards—so the original engineers had cut some corners. Whenever they wrote the date, for instance, they had abbreviated the four numbers of the year, using only the last two. As the year 2000 approached, programmers began to wonder whether computers would interpret the abbreviated "00" as 1900, rather than 2000. If that occurred, what would happen to the entire network? Would everything shut down?

There were lots of opinions and reassurances, but no one knew for sure until the moment actually arrived. As it turned out, everything was fine, and the band played on some more. But the moment, which soon became a remembered joke as if no one was ever really worried, was palpable and real.

Symbolically, a new era had arisen. A fresh millennium was upon us. New Year's resolutions were a little more meaningful that time around. The 20th century had ended. The 21st had begun. It was going to be all good from here on out!

But resolutions are funny things. You can resolve to start an exercise regimen, for example, and even hit the gym a time or two, but the old habits that prompted the resolutions are still at work. Sloth dies hard, and enthusiasm wanes quickly. The old stream of dirty water continues to flow into the future, and it refuses to be diverted by a simple decision. You have to work at it.

Anyone who has ever tried to quit smoking knows that sad but powerful truth. I had an old friend who once told me quitting cigarettes was easy. He had done it a hundred times. It was staying free of the old habit that was so difficult.

America had managed to cover over a lot of social problems in the 1990s, but many cultural habits were still there below the surface. They hadn't disappeared; they had merely gone underground. And they would soon surface with a vengeance. A decade-and-a-half later, in the presidential elections of 2016 and 2020, they would blossom anew. Racism, misogyny, political greed, and the lust for power sprang forth into the light of day.

It was not a pretty sight.

As I write these words in 2022, the future of American democracy is very much in doubt. This was unheard of in 2000. Back then, today's news headlines would have been seen as beyond any realm of possibility. Climate conditions that threaten coastal cities and spark extreme weather were thought to be something we didn't have to worry about for a hundred years. Terrorism at today's scale was hardly on anyone's radar. At least not within the boundaries of our country. That was something that only occurred far away, on foreign soil to people who weren't as "sophisticated" and "civilized" as us. The thought of a 9/11 hadn't entered anyone's mind until just a short 21 months later. Although I sincerely and fervently hope that by the time you read these words the threat will have abated, the headlines I read this morning proclaimed that we were on the verge of World War III. Unthinkable!

In turn-of-the-century America, we thought we had introduced laws that ensured voting rights, civil rights, gay rights, and women's rights. We were a nation of laws, we thought, and once they were enshrined in legal-ese, the problems were rectified for good.

So, when the slight worry of total collapse at midnight passed on that momentous New Year celebration, and the new millennium began, we partied on. It was business as usual. "As it was in the beginning, so is it now and ever shall be. World without end!" Let the good times continue to roll!

What was going on in the nation as a whole was mirrored in my life. Having experimented with living a more normal life, making money, playing the game, and having been burned in the process, I had for a time retreated into the old lifestyle. But old habits die hard. I still longed for money, recognition, and security. I still wondered how I was going to pay the bills. I still kept on keeping on, the way most of us do.

Meanwhile, the world was changing. Facebook was launched in 2004, Twitter in 2007. Instagram was to follow in 2010, and Snapchat in 2011. Social media was about to take over the world. Instant communication. Every person would soon have their own platform. Cell phones and hand-held gadgets were everywhere.

Little did we know that they were the vanguard of a questionable revolution. Technology always offers enticing temptations. It's fun when good guys like us use it, but we didn't realize what could happen when bad guys learned the rules.

Me? I joined in the social revolution, too, in my own way. I got married. My wife, Barb, and I built a house together. I worked a bunch of part-time jobs and did a lot of hunting and fishing. I was the pastor of a small church. I wrote a book. I taught college courses. It was just like the old days.

As I said, though, old habits die hard. Society places a real burden on even well-meaning, aging folks. Maybe especially on well-meaning, aging folks, who, as they age, get tired more easily. Money again reared its ugly head. Doesn't it always? A young man such as I once was can resist, make do, and hold out. But after a while, you get weary. Economic burdens become too heavy to bear.

Barb and I gave it a go. We sold the new house, paid off as many bills as we could, moved into a travel trailer full time, and relocated all the way to Arizona. I took on another part-time church job in a new environment. A nice environment, to be sure, but we soon discovered we couldn't escape society. It will wear you down wherever you go.

I had hoped that learning how to live and thrive in a totally new place would help. It used to, but after a few close calls in the desert, where mistakes can kill you (and almost did a few times), it soon became obvious that in ways both physical and emotional I was no longer as young as I used to be.

Perhaps it came to a head one lonely day when I sat in my office, hoping to soon connect with the church treasurer and my monthly paycheck so I could have a few bucks to put enough gas in the car to get home. She never showed up. I called her. She wasn't coming. The church wouldn't have enough money to pay me until next week. I was stuck.

Oh, I had been in that position before. I should have expected it, but somehow, this time was too much. I just couldn't cope any more. I needed to go back to work at a full-time church with a full-time paycheck and a full-time grind and accept whatever emotional problems that entailed. Against my better judgment, I rejoined the ranks of those who played by the rules.

That day, in my lonely office, I hit rock bottom and capitulated to the inevitable. I gave up and decided I had to return to the establishment.

I finally admitted defeat.

They had won.

THE QUESTION

Is any of it real, or is it just a big game?

I can't emphasize enough what all this was doing to my spiritual life. It's hard for a minister to admit it, but when you're dealing with basic survival in a secular society you just can't put yourself in a framework conducive to spiritual growth. At least, I can't. There is a reason monks, nuns, gurus, shamans, and holy men and women down through the ages went on perpetual retreats. When you are constantly worried about where the next car payment is coming from, it's hard to concentrate enough to get yourself in a mental position to discover spiritual truths, let alone meet the "Source of All That Is."

In the course of my life, I have talked to thousands of people about discernment and spiritual growth and often wondered why most people don't seem to really care, aside from professing a casual interest, in the beliefs and activities that have constituted my Holy Grail. I have pondered far into the night about the lack of passion for mystery in our culture. Where is the desire for magic? Where is the burning interest in spirituality?

What I was coming to believe is that popular culture, far from promoting these topics, has either ignored them or treated them with an element of patronizing belittlement.

Although there is evidence that things may finally be changing, at least in some quarters, why has this been the dominating tendency, even though we traditionally call ourselves a religious people?

One of the reasons, I was beginning to understand as the decade unfolded, was that spiritual maturity is, of necessity, the specialty of elders. They are the ones who have had the most experience, the most time to think, and the most years to observe and develop wisdom.

We have now, for the most part, eliminated the icon of the valued elder. What have we put in its place? The image of a tech-savvy child who came of age during the dot-com bubble of the late '90s.

The bottom line is this: In western society we now worship youth. I realize that's quite a statement, but think about it for a minute. Try this exercise. Watch a few hours of TV and jot down the content of the commercials you see. What you will find is this:

- Our culture constantly bombards us with the supposed necessity of buying the latest technological toys in order to "be cool." Smart phones, GPS devices, tablets, and on and on. If you want to get ahead you have to be savvy about such things. AARP even cautions its members to get technologically relevant or they'll never be able to communicate with their kids. Let's call these devices what they are. Toys! And who plays with toys? Children!

- Our culture constantly bombards us with the supposed necessity of appearing young. Ads for cosmetics, skin care products, and clothing fill the airwaves. "You're only as young as you feel!" "Make love like a youngster!" "Stay youthful so you can play games." "Buy a cool car and feel young again!" Who is interested in these kinds of advertised goodies? Who places great emphasis on looks, sex, games, and possessions? Children!

- Our culture constantly bombards us with the supposed necessity of keeping busy. Work three jobs. Never retire. Multitask. Look at your email and Twitter accounts. Get involved with social media. Check in with friends. Never sit quietly in a chair and reflect because it will slow you down. Listen to tunes while you catch up on the latest fashion trends. Memorize the lyrics and the exotic names of performers. Do more. Move faster. Don't stop or life will overtake you. Who attacks life with such hyperactive frenzy? Children!

It's hard for a young person to really, existentially, believe they are going to die. Oh, they understand the fact of death, but they don't believe deep down in their souls that it will ever happen to them. It's an intellectually imagined reality that is easily pushed aside when in the prime of life. I was guilty of it when I was young, and so were you. That's probably why we were all capable of doing some pretty dangerous things, whether it involved driving too fast, taking some fierce drugs, or participating in outlandish activities. Outcomes weren't quite real, somehow, so deep and abiding spiritual growth wasn't something we were really interested in.

Besides, when we were young, we thought we knew everything. It became a habit, and many people sustained that habit throughout their entire lifetime.

In our culture it is common to never even bring up the subject of death, except in jest. Although it happens to us all, it's considered morbid. As a minister, of course, I often led funeral services—sometimes as often as a few times every week—so I suppose I grew used to it. But I am constantly surprised to meet people who have never seen a dead body until they are well along in life. And even then, it's usually after it has been cleaned for viewing in a funeral home or church.

And yet death is a common staple of our entertainment. Virtually every episode of the nightly barrage of TV cop shows begins with a gruesome death scene. Most video games are all about death and destruction. It's as though we're pretending death doesn't exist except as entertainment, even though we know it does. Perhaps it's a part of our culture for just that reason. We fear it so much we attempt to trivialize it by saturating ourselves with it in the form of fantasy.

I bring this up because in all my years of talking to people about spiritual growth I have found only one, sure-fire, absolute, certain technique that will induce people to do an about-face when it comes to contemplating the reality of death and what comes next. That method has many variations, but the most common is a diagnosis of an incurable disease such as cancer. Nothing makes a person look seriously at life more than being forced to admit that it's going to end.

The plain and simple fact is this: Someday, each and every one of us, without exception, will learn whether or not God and the afterlife--or whatever else we want to call it—exist. Current spiritual mysteries will become our reality—our new home. Psychic experiences will no longer be a mere intellectual exercise. Scientific truths will be proved to be either profound or silly. If we exist in a multiverse, that multiverse will become our new playground.

"In my Father's house are many rooms," Jesus was reported to have said in John 14:2. At death we will come to know if those "many rooms" are metaphors, or entire universes, or if they even exist at all. To quote yet another Bible verse, "For now we see only a reflection, as in a mirror; then we shall see face to face. Now I know in part; then I shall know fully, even as I am fully known" (I Corinthians 13:2).

I have just quoted Christian scripture verses because they are familiar to most people. You hear them a lot at funerals. But every sacred text of every great religion says similar things when you begin to open the pages and read what has been there for thousands of years, recorded for all to see. Life after death is a concept that goes back to the very first humans who placed flowers and tools in the graves of their loved ones. You don't do such a thing unless you believe they will serve a future purpose for the one who has passed on.

I once stood at the bedside of a friend who had founded a college, enjoyed a successful teaching career, served in various local political offices, and made a small fortune along the way. He was also a deacon in the church and had the reputation of being a well-respected pillar in the community. I was there because I had received a late-night phone call from a nurse at the local hospital. My friend was dying and was not expected to live out the night. He had asked for me, so of course I got out of bed and quickly made my way to be with him.

I found him in tears. I asked if he was ready to cross over, and he said something I will never forget: "Jim, for my whole life I have done everything but the one thing that was most important. I never prepared for this moment."

We were lucky. He made it through that long night and lasted for ten more. I spent a few hours of every one of those next days with him. I hope I was able to help. I don't know if I taught him anything. I know he taught me a lot.

This story illustrates the fact that we all live one heartbeat away from the reality of spiritual enlightenment—one heartbeat away from the goal of my lifetime quest. Yet the modern lifestyle we have invented prevents us from really taking the time to contemplate it. We spend more time teaching our children algebra than we do preparing them for the end of their life.

We need to look deep within ourselves in order to understand that it is only in the realm of the soul that we can look with eyes attuned to the spirit rather than the illusion that seems so very, very solid but has proven to be just that—an illusion. That's tough to do in a shallow, materialistic society.

There is a lot more to life than many of us have ever contemplated—a greater mystery than we often realize. Perhaps we may someday—after death inevitably claims us if not before--come to see that this particular quest is the most important task we can undertake in life. Maybe it's even the reason why, assuming we had some choice in the matter, we chose to be born in the first place. Maybe it's the reason we are alive.

Ultimately, who knows for sure? We live deep within the foggy illusion that surrounds us and pervades our very being—the illusion that "what we see is what we get." But that is precisely the illusion that came to fruition during the decade of the '90s and persisted full-blown into the new millennium.

It abides with us still.

Chapter 7:
Free at Last (the 21st Century)

THE CULTURE

Maturity rears its blessed head. The Grail reveals itself. And it appears in a form I never expected.

By the end of the first decade of the 21st century, I had spent 40 years in Christian ministry, 50 years as a part-time professional musician, 45 years as a public-school teacher and then a college professor, and a long time as an on-again/off-again carpenter. Along the way, I had written some books that dealt wholly, or at least partially, with the quest for spirituality in the midst of a very materialistic culture.

By Labor Day of 2009, I was ready to hang it up, but even in retirement I had a goal. My bucket list was pretty well checked off. I had hiked a good deal of the Appalachian Trail, using the trail name of my alter ego, Rip Walker, and pedaled a bicycle for more miles than I can remember. I'd ventured forth alone on bike trips that took me from the Pacific to the Atlantic and from Florida to Massachusetts. Because rivers always fascinated me, I had biked the length of the Connecticut, the Millers, the St. Johns, and the Savannah and paddled a canoe down many of the great rivers of Michigan and Maine, not to mention the Erie Canal. I'd hunted caribou in the wilderness of Quebec, ruffed grouse in the Adirondacks, pheasants in New York back in the days when the cornfields went on forever, deer from Florida's panhandle to New England, squirrels in Massachusetts, turkeys in New Hampshire, and rabbits

More miles than I can remember. — Port Orange, FL (2007, photo by Bob Brewster).

Biking the Savannah River — South Carolina (2012).

Hiking. — Western MA (mid-1970s).

Concert with the trombone section of the Los Angeles Symphony — Alabama and Georgia (2006).

in Michigan. I'd had the good luck to fish all over the place, spend a lot of time alone in the woods, and enjoy the friendship of many wonderful people.

In many ways I'd lived a fulfilling life and done pretty much everything I ever dreamed of doing. But when I retired from it all there was one more thing I wanted to accomplish. It had always been my goal to live for one year in the woods, cut off from people in general, so I could watch the leaves change colors with the passing seasons. During that time, I wanted to experience God.

I told myself that if the prophets of old could speak to God and have God speak back to them, I saw no reason why I couldn't do it as well. I was ready to pay any price, do whatever needed doing, and learn whatever there was to learn. I even had a Bible verse in mind that I was going to claim as my own. Using words attributed to Jacob of old as he wrestled with God all night, my soul cried out, "I will not let you go until you bless me!"

That one year has turned into more than a decade, so far. And, lo and behold, my prayer was answered. God didn't appear in Christian garb. I suppose that would never have worked. After a lifetime as a clergyman, the words and concepts of my religious tradition had probably acquired too much familiar baggage. No, God appeared in a form consistent with my surroundings here in the woods—the world's oldest religion and spiritual tradition: pagan shamanism. Out of the mists of that which has, in many circles, been disparaged as superstitious metaphysics or the paranormal, I discovered meaning and wholeness. And if that wasn't enough, my lifetime love of science, which had matured with a layman's study of quantum physics and the challenging but exciting ideas of Ervin Lazlo's Akashic Field Theory, kept pace in wondrous fashion. In short, I discovered the identity of God.

It began in an unexpected way.

I woke up on the second Sunday of September 2009 with a strange feeling inside. It was Sunday, and I wasn't going to church. It was September, and I didn't need to think about planning for a busy fall schedule. Tomorrow was Monday, and I didn't need to go to school to teach any classes. My trombone was safely tucked away in its case, and I didn't need to get it out in order to keep my embouchure in shape for any upcoming gigs.

I glanced at the calendar next to the phone. My first appointment was three months away. I tuned into the sounds of morning. No cars, no traffic, no neighbors. Just the sounds of the dawn chorus of birds.

What did I need to do today?

Nothing!

For a few minutes I had a hard time adjusting. Even now, more than a decade later, I must confess that I'm still not used to it. If, on a Sunday morning, I know there's someplace I need to be next Thursday, unless I catch myself, I'll fret about it all week long. On the rare occasions I come in to find the light on the answering machine blinking, I tend to panic because I feel there must be something wrong. Then I press the button and discover a message from a telemarketer.

I don't own a cell phone, except for the throwaway Barb insists I carry with me on long bike trips. I wouldn't even do that if there were any pay phones still available. I recently learned my phone also takes pictures. I'll have to learn how to do that someday. Maybe.

All this is to say that it's hard to leave a society that is so wired, so plugged in, so constantly moving, so connected, and so stressful that most people don't even realize it until, like me, they try to step outside it for a while. Then it becomes apparent. Something has gone horribly wrong. It feels to me, especially now that I've been out in the woods and separate from people for so many years now, as though we were never meant to live in such close and hectic contact. Most of us will never admit it, even to ourselves, while we're swept up in it, but I've found it to be true.

I've had folks disagree and argue with me about this. Usually, the only way to prove my point is to challenge them to unplug for a week. I've yet to have anyone take me up on it.

An alcoholic might swear he can give up booze whenever he wants, but he rarely wants to do it. Likewise, an overly stressed, techno-addict will swear he can get rid of his devices, turn off his TV, and unplug his phone whenever he wants, but he never quite finds a convenient time to try it.

Here's the thing: Over the years, I've learned that it takes long periods of uninterrupted time to contemplate the important questions of life. To be honest, it's hard and lonely work.

I've had people tell me that when they get stressed, they take a half-hour walk to calm down. But take it from someone who has lived for more than a decade in an almost constant state of meditation, a half-hour walk around the block will not affect a cure. At best, it's a band-aid. It's a good thing to do, but it's not enough. Not nearly enough.

Great art, great ideas, great music, and great poetry arise from the Muse, or consciousness, or God, or the Akashic Field, or whatever else you want to call it. And the secret to accessing that Source is time, solitude, and, I firmly believe, nature.

That statement demands some explanation. From the first appearance of simple matter to the solid formation of rock and hill; from the fires of Mother Earth's warm heart to the cold of her polar ice; from the smallest, one-celled amoeba to the greatest of the stolid land creatures, the continuing theme of nature seems to be survival of the fittest. Only the strong and best adapted survive to reproduce. Nature "red in tooth and claw" seems to dominate our environment. It is the law that drives evolution.

But what about beauty and love? Where did they come from? Can we find love in the constant battle for the survival of the fittest? Does love exist in untimely death—indeed, in death at all? In the long evolutionary march of creation, can love survive betrayal and war, inhumanity and brutality?

Creatures of time and space will probably answer with a resounding "NO!" Those who believe that Alpha and Omega, "Beginning" and "End," anchor two ends of a straight arrow of time cannot conceive of such a thing. But to the person who knows

Alpha and Omega inhabit identical, overlapping points on a great circle; to someone who suspects that the beginning and the end are one and the same; to one who sees not the past and future, but only the ever-present and eternal *Now*, love permeates creation. Gaia knows. To live is to love. Consciousness sings the song. Energy writes the music. Love is the theme.

So it is that even as Gaia endures the crucifixion of pavement and strip mall; even as the nails of industrial mining pierce her flesh, and the crown of thorny development is pressed upon her bowed head; even as rivers of her polluted blood empty into life-giving waters, from the very brink of death her call goes forth in love, "Forgive them! They know not what they do."

That, my friends, is love!

But to hear that message we need time, space, quiet, solitude, and nature.

Let me share an example we experienced shortly after we moved to the woods.

It began, as such things often do, with a bump in the night. When you live at the end of a lonely, self-constructed road, surrounded by dark forest containing not even a hint of artificial light or human sounds, a bump in the night immediately sets your hackles to rise. Barbara and I paused in unison, waiting to see what might come next. But … nothing. So, we relaxed and went to bed.

With dawn came the tragic answer to last night's mystery—a discovery that broke our hearts. A female cardinal, confused by the dwindling light of the last few minutes of dusk and the intrusion of the new porch we just finished that day, had flown into the screen, broken her neck, and instantly died. If that weren't enough to shake us to the core, her bright-red mate had chosen to remain faithful to her right up until the end. His allegiance cost him his life. We couldn't tell why he was flopping around on the porch. Perhaps it was a broken wing. Possibly internal injuries. Maybe even a broken heart. All we knew was that he was hurting badly and very frightened.

Little cardinals, your beauty cannot die. — Plum Branch, SC (2008)

We placed him in a towel-lined box, gave him food, water, and words of comfort, and hoped for the best. He made it through the long day and even longer night, but it became painfully obvious to us that he would soon join his mate in that place where beauty such as theirs remains eternally safe and secure, free from the tragedies of this plane of existence.

Strange, isn't it? A cardinal, despite its outward beauty, is no more worthy of praise than any other bird. Red plumage doesn't somehow bestow nobility upon its host. Surely a small brown sparrow is as much a miracle as any other bird, whether that bird be red, blue, or orange. But somehow, seeing two sleek bodies, one a brilliant red and one a more subtle hue of scarlet and brown, lying lifeless on our deck caused us both to fall into a deep depression.

If it is true that birds descended from dinosaurs, as more and more evidence suggests, then they have been around in various evolutionary incarnations for millions of years. Even an asteroid could not kill off their kind. They simply adapted, through fire and famine, tragedy and mayhem, and learned to roll with life's punches. They arose from the ashes of defeat and resurrected to new life.

Until, that is, they encountered the works of our hands. It was our screen porch that brought them down. And our guilt was palpable. We had built the porch, in part, so that we could sit outside on warm summer evenings and watch the very birds that now lay dead at our feet.

No amount of consolation could cheer us up that day. Each of us tried to humor the other but to no avail. We were disconsolate, and only time would help assuage our grief. When we buried them, there seemed to be only one place that would do.

There is a special spot of ground where we greet each and every sunrise—indeed, where we mark the passing of times and seasons, the place where each day begins anew for us.

Perhaps, again, an explanation is in order.

If it is true that confession is good for the soul then I, a retired minister, have a confession to make. I haven't been inside a church for years now, ever since I pronounced the benediction at my final service and waltzed off into retirement. There has never been a time in my entire life when I have stayed away this long.

This is not to say that I turned my back on God, or "Cosmo," as Barb and I sometimes call the great Mystery that has occupied my every waking thought for more than 70 years.

But much to our surprise, we became quite pagan. We discovered meaning behind every sunrise and sunset. We began to sense the connectedness that binds every living thing. We experienced a Sacred Moment each morning when we discovered new deer tracks on the paths we walked at sunrise.

The indigenous people of New England, where we used to live, called it *Manitou*—Mystery. We don't know what the first people to live here, on this spot of ground, called it. But we came to

*Watching the sunrise has become
quite a ritual for us.*

understand, through discovering the artifacts they left behind, that
they must have had their own descriptive name.

We watched the changing seasons and acknowledged them by
raising standing stones to mark the place where the sun finishes its

journey to the north or south at the solstices. Many mornings we stand above a flat rock in back of our house. It has become quite a ritual for us. There are mornings when the sun shines red and purple against a hazel-blue sky, the first birds begin to sing, the squirrels begin their busy day, and we sense the Power that was here long before we humans first walked this earth.

At such moments we discover that to be made in the image of God means that ours was the first species to evolve both art and a vocabulary sufficient to attempt a description of nature. Our Trinity consists of the *Consciousness* behind the creation, the *Beauty* of its outward form, and the *Power* that binds it together. Such a trinity cannot be contained in a building, or even within a community. Indeed, these things sometimes hinder more than help.

(One morning, Barb remarked, "We need some kind of ritual prayer to say as we stand here and begin the day." Then she immediately grinned, looked at me, and said, "That's how it starts, isn't it?" She was, of course, talking about religion. We still laugh about it.)

All this is to say that we felt there was only one place to bury the beautiful, miraculous creatures who paid the ultimate sacrifice for our moving into what, until recently, had been their domain. We took them out back and buried them beneath the stone, where we often stand each morning to watch the sunrise.

And there they stayed as the days went by. We didn't forget them, but we learned to live with their loss. Our troubled spirits sought to make sense out of what seemed a senseless death. It was a small tragedy, I suppose, in the great scheme of things. It didn't rank up there with war and famine, earthquake, flood, and hurricane. After all, what was the difference between two dead birds and the mice I sometimes kill in my mousetraps when they break the treaty we made with them when we moved in? ("You get the outside—We get the inside!")

But it was *our* tragedy, however small. And it moved us deeply.

That was how things stood as the days passed and our musings continued through the cold, dark days of our first pagan winter.

And make no mistake about it, those days were dark. During our first few months here in the silence of the woods we kept ourselves busy—probably out of habit. We had buildings to raise, landscaping to accomplish, and a new life to begin. Our days of achievement and public work had, we thought, ended. It was time to begin a new stage of life—one of appreciation and wonder. We were moving on, filling our days with activity. We didn't have much time to think deep thoughts. But we carried with us quite a lot of baggage and, much to our surprise, we are still learning how to shed ourselves of its weight.

Some of that baggage is, yes, bitterness. During my career as a minister, I tried to help people open themselves up to the life of the spirit. The great majority of those in my congregations never even began to suspect what I was talking about. I retired with words attributed to Jesus ringing in my head:

We had buildings to raise.... First construction in South Carolina (2007).

O Jerusalem, you who stone the prophets and kill those God sends to you, how often I have wanted to gather you under my wings as a mother hen gathers her chicks. But you would not!

—Matthew 23:37

Hubris, perhaps? Certainly! Puffed up with my own importance? Of course! A task too big for any one man to take on? Sure!

But it hurts just the same. It hurts to be misunderstood. It hurts to be frustrated when the institution to which you have devoted your life misunderstands its calling again and again, falling short of even the simplest commands of its founder.

I have watched my beloved denomination, along with many others, shrink in size, influence, and understanding. I've seen future pastors go to seminary for all the wrong reasons. I've seen clergy drown in a sea of politics. I've heard musicians raise their voices only for personal glory. I've seen people with absolutely no sense of spirituality rise to positions of leadership in the church— the blind leading the blind. I've seen those who cannot foster a spiritual life reduce the impact of mission to simple acts of charity. I've stood at the bedsides of too many people who realized, too late, that they were not prepared to make their final journey. "How often I have wanted to gather you in…. But you would not!"

Stepping away after those many years slowly rendered a change. I hardly think the transformation is complete. But this one thing I seem to have learned: It's no secret that Christianity embraced a lot of pagan ritual.

Any holy day—Easter, for instance—that features an outside service at sunrise on the first Sunday following the first full moon after the spring equinox, throws in some ancient fertility symbols like chickens and eggs, and perhaps even (at least in English) names itself after the goddess Ishtar, cannot be any further removed from paganism than two people who raise standing stones and greet the sun each morning.

Truth is a multifaceted, bright, shining gem. At different times, in different places, in different ways, human beings have gazed upon that gem, glimpsing a reflection of its glory in one of its many facets. Our problem is that we have, too often, mistaken the particular facet that engaged our attention for the complete reality. We have built institutions that reflect the glory of a single facet and miss the rich totality of the shining truth of the whole.

The eternal beauty of Truth is that it refuses to be buried beneath the decaying constructs of us mortals. We may become bitter and, in our selfish, misguided anger, feel that Truth is buried for good, too deep to be resurrected. At such times we shake our fist at our institutions and cry, "Let them all die! Burn them all down!" But like the dinosaurs who rolled with the punches and were transformed into beautiful, red cardinals to face a new age of mammals made in the image of God, the essential Truth of God refuses to be buried beneath the rubble of human works, institutions, and apathy.

All world religions teach the same things. They all speak of sacrifice that leads to new life and understanding. They teach the essential truths of death and resurrection. They admit the reality of human sin but teach that there is new life at the end of the cold, dark, winter. Spring is always a time of resurrection and new life.

I thought of these things one morning as Barb and I stood to watch the sunrise. We talked about the need to prepare ourselves for the blossoming of spring at the equinox. We spoke about our need to spend time contemplating the new life that is birthing anew within and around us. We looked forward together to the bursting forth of the buds and flowers of spring and the work that lay before us in preparing the gardens and gathering the harvest.

As always, we thought about the bodies of the beautiful birds that lay dead and buried at our feet—that gave their lives in sacrifice to we who wanted nothing more than to appreciate their world and who eagerly awaited the return of their sons and daughters with the coming of the warm and bright tomorrow of summer.

In that moment, we realized that it was the eve of Ash Wednesday, the first day of Lent, and we felt a bit sheepish. All this "new stuff" we were discussing had been there all along, during my career as a minister. All the ritual, all the symbolism, all the metaphor. Christians call it Lent.

I had never spent much time thinking about it. My preparations were always for the *next* study series, the *next* sermon, the *next* church service. I had understood it with my head but not my heart. It took paganism to teach me the truths of my own religion. It took moving away from the busy world of people for me to come to understand that the church is merely one present-day incarnation of a much older Truth—the Truth that will continue long after we feeble humans have been buried in the dust along with our petty arguments and disagreements.

Ray Stevens used to sing, "There is none so blind as he who will not see." The Sacrifice goes on forever. The beauty that found metaphorical expression in our two cardinals will not, indeed *cannot*, be buried, covered over with a stone, and forgotten.

Gloria Gaither once wrote, "The purest water is the stream that bursts crystal clear into the sunlight after it has forced its way through solid rock."

"Fear not, little flock," said Jesus.

Little cardinals—your beauty cannot die. Your life is forever.

If birds can make you think thoughts such as these, are they not messengers from nature itself? That is why in shamanic tradition, animals—both in spirit and in flesh, in dreams and in actual encounters—are seen as threshold guardians. They stand at the point of contact between the world of nature and the spirit.

I probably didn't grasp the significance of it at the time, but there are lessons that go far beyond superficial beauty. Can nature find words extensive enough to teach us those lessons? If so, how can she speak to us in language we can understand? If only we could find a way to meet Gaia halfway. What stories she could share!

THE QUESTION

Is a rich spirituality even possible until after you've lived a full life?

As I recounted earlier, way back in my early twenties I turned to the church as a nourishing womb within which I could nurture a life of spirituality.

I was disappointed. It didn't happen. What spiritual gains I made came about more *in spite of* the church than *because* of it.

Sad to say, that situation hasn't changed very much with the passage of time. The church is dwindling, and, I'm sorry to say, justifiably so. During the last few decades especially, my original home brand, the Evangelical church, and later the liberal, main-stream variety of Protestantism that was my place of service for 30 years, has fallen on bad times.

We should have seen it coming back in 1980. As a matter of fact, some of us did, but we were powerless to do much about it. Jimmy Carter, an Evangelical Baptist Sunday school teacher, and as fine a man as Christianity has ever produced, found himself facing Ronald Regan's bid for the presidency. Carter was a Democrat. Regan a Republican. After serving one term as president, Carter had run out of time before he could get the hostage situation in Iran cleared up. Many say that cost him the election.

But what really defeated him was the fact that his own religious community, the Evangelical church, abandoned him. Why? The answer was simple. Ever since the acknowledged Evangelical leader, Jerry Falwell, a Baptist himself, had persuaded his so-called "moral majority" that politics was more important than religious faith and had introduced secular power into the equation of American Christianity, the church has turned more and more political with each passing voting cycle. In the second decade of the 21ˢᵗ century, that policy tore the church in half.

It came to a head in the election of 2016. Donald Trump hardly ever set foot in a church until he ran for president. His lying and cheating had already become legendary.

Trump's abuse of women was, by his own admission when caught on a live microphone, abominable. But he was embraced by the Evangelical church anyway. He was, according to church leaders, "a leaky vessel." But he was *God's* leaky vessel, they said. After all, King David was a sinner, too. As was Solomon himself, when it came to his attitude toward women.

Evangelical church leaders had been given the keys to the kingdom in Washington, D.C., when it became apparent that they commanded a big voting bloc. Evangelical leaders gloried in having lunch with the president. The church had gained the whole world. But in doing so, it had lost its soul.

The faithful began to leave the church in droves, not because *they* no longer believed what the church traditionally taught, but because the *church* had stopped believing in what the church traditionally taught. Their numbers were replaced by those who saw conservative religion as a gateway to political power. Jerry Falwell had once said, "We need to get people saved and registered to vote!" A few decades later, by early 2020, pastors were urging their congregations to "keep their Bible open and their guns loaded!"

Back in the early '80s, I received an urgent call one morning from someone connected to a big outdoor venue in New Hampshire, just north of where I lived, called The Cathedral in the Pines. Charles Colson, who was labeled "Nixon's Hatchet Man" during the Watergate trials, had been convicted for his role in that infamous Republican plot to subvert an election. After his release from prison, he had converted to Christianity and gone on to build a very effective prison ministry called Crossroads.

Colson was scheduled to speak that morning at the outdoor Cathedral, but the music group that was to open for him, for reasons I don't remember, was a no-show. Could my wife and I come up right away and fill in at the last minute?

A chance to see Charles Colson in person? Sure! So we packed up my guitars and drove up right away.

By the time we got there a crowd had already started to gather. It would soon grow to about a thousand people. Our job was to keep them entertained with gospel music until the main event started.

After a quick introduction, we were on. But Colson was late, so what had been scheduled for a few tunes turned into a full hour-and-a-half concert. When Colson finally arrived and walked down the center aisle, he had obviously been told what had happened because he gave us a covert thumbs-up sign and a big smile when he reached the front and we finished our set.

After he finished his inspirational speech, full of insider in-formation about what went on within the confines of the Oval Office, we were packing up to go home when a messenger arrived with an invitation. Colson and his entourage were having lunch at the home of a wealthy patron nearby. It was to be a catered af-fair featuring fresh lobster flown in that morning from the nearby coast. He wanted us to attend if at all possible, so he could thank us personally.

Having nothing scheduled on our calendar that was more in-teresting than a personal meeting with a Nixon insider, who was now a biggie in conservative church circles, we decided to go.

When we got there, we found an elaborate outdoor picnic in full swing. We went through the food line, filled up our plates with all kinds of exotic delicacies, found an empty table, and sat down. Colson must have been looking for us. Within a minute he came over and asked to join us. We soon found ourselves engaged in a fascinating conversation with a very intelligent, well-spoken man, who was surprisingly easy to talk to.

I can't remember everything that was said that day, but one sto-ry stands out. Colson told us how easy it had been in the old days to get the White House message out to the Evangelical church. Mega churches were blooming all over the country. The White House would issue dinner invitations to a few influential televan-gelists, such as Jerry Falwell, from Thomas Road Baptist Church in Lynchburg, or James Kennedy, from Coral Ridge Presbyterian Church in Fort Lauderdale.

After an afternoon basking in front of TV cameras in the White House, the guests would be treated to a voyage down the Potomac on the presidential yacht, *Sequoia*. The event would be carefully

timed so as to float by the U.S. Naval Academy, near Annapolis, at sundown. The flag was lowered each day at that hour, and the invited guests would all stand on deck, hands over their hearts, against the backdrop of the setting sun as "Taps" was sounded by the bugler. Someone would invariably be asked to lead in prayer. It was always an emotional time, and the White House chief of staff could be sure that next Sunday morning, every one of these megachurch leaders would faithfully, during the course of their televised sermon, relate every one of the talking points they had been surreptitiously fed over the course of their visit.

Evangelical leaders, Colson assured us, were the easiest constituents to bamboozle.

The so-called liberal church wasn't any better. Politics had long ago invaded their ranks as well. Without the heartfelt conviction of their more conservative brethren, they had convinced themselves that devotion to Jesus had to be displayed through works of charity to "the least of these, my brethren," as the Bible so aptly put it. Liberal churches preferred high-fallutin' music by Bach and Beethoven over the foot-stompin' gospel tunes played in the church down the street, but they were no less emotional when it came time to brush shoulders with the political elite who held real power in the United States.

A new generation of the rich and powerful had almost completely taken over the reins of influence, and they were beginning to understand the power of what would soon become known as social media. The church had, for the most part, moved away from its mission to nurture spiritual growth and faith. Conservatives relied more and more on raw emotion, while liberals concentrated on academic intellectualism, but the result was the same. People no longer found what they were looking for on Sunday morning, and church membership began to plummet.

That was the case when I finally decided to hang it up and retire to the woods. I had good intentions about wrestling with God, I just didn't know how. I somehow knew that formal prayers and the kind of academic study I had engaged throughout my life wouldn't do. But I didn't know what would replace it. I felt that somehow nature had to be involved in the process, but I certainly wasn't a shamanic pagan.

Yet!

It was in trying to figure all this out that I made the discovery that changed everything. Having spent so much time alone in the woods throughout my life, I had often felt what can only be called a spiritual thrill when I entered an old oak grove, stood at the crest of a mountain, or contemplated a babbling brook. I was vaguely aware that there were energies inherent in the earth itself—energies that create and sustain material existence. I recognized that there are forces embedded within every natural process, from the migration patterns of birds and butterflies to the latest research results culminating in the discovery of the so-called "God particle" at the Large Hadron Collider near Geneva, Switzerland.

Our ancestors, being as much a product of evolutionary forces as birds and butterflies, lived much closer to nature than we do now and recognized the effect these energies had upon them. They called them spirit guides, fairy folk, leprechauns, angels, or "little people." They looked upon them as messengers of the gods.

The Dragon, often called *Serpent* in the West, is a universal metaphor for Earth energy. "Dragon Lines" and "Paths of the Serpent" were once well known. Their routes, vortexes, and convergence spots were often marked by pillars, stone circles, and monoliths. Stonehenge is probably the best-known example, situated as it is just south of the Michael and Mary "Serpent Lines," probably the most well-documented energy leys in all of England. Their course is marked by many famous standing stones and holy places, including Glastonbury and Avebury.

The rise of Western science cast most of these ideas into the dustbin of mythology and superstition, but the underlying Earth energies continued to manifest their existence to a few who followed the old ways. Australian Aborigine elders still claim to see a landscape seamed with energy lines. Even in this day and age, modern contractors in Hawaii make it a practice to consult with

Stonehenge

respected experts called *kahunas* before orienting new buildings. New York businesses sometimes call upon a Chinese tradition by hiring *feng shui* masters to design office spaces. Many well drillers will not move their equipment into position until a sensitive old-timer surveys the area with dowsing rods or a forked willow branch. Police departments quietly employ dowsers who search for lost people with high-resolution topographical maps and a swinging pendulum.

In short, as I was soon to discover, the phenomenon of Earth energy has not gone away. Indeed, published results in disparate fields, from modern theoretical physics to DNA research in migrating butterflies, seem to describe a mathematical, observable, and repeatable quantum reality our ancestors would readily recognize as central to their core experience.

I had not yet come to understand all this. I just somehow felt it. That's how I came to experiment with the art of dowsing. I wrote about this in my self-published book, *The Dragon Awakes*. But since that book never sold more than 50 copies, and isn't even in print anymore, I have no problem sharing my experience pretty much verbatim as I first wrote about it.

For many years I had been skeptical of folks who searched for water with rods or willow sticks. I had watched a few dowsers at their work, seen the rods or stick move or plunge downward, and tried to figure out how they were doing it. I had been told that some well-drilling companies won't even drive to a property without hiring a "water witch" to tell them if there's water present and where to drill. But I thought it was all poppycock.

Nevertheless, one day I decided to try it myself. Why? I don't have the faintest idea. One moment I was a skeptic. The next, I wanted to try it.

After doing some Internet research (we don't do anything these days without Internet research, do we?), I decided the simplest way to get started was to get some brass rods, bend them into what are called "L-rods," and see if it worked.

I didn't dare tell my wife, Barbara, what I was doing, so I just quietly made a surreptitious trip to the local hardware store. They didn't have any brass rods, so I got some solid copper wire in the heaviest gauge I could get, cut it into two 18-inch pieces, bent them into a shape roughly like the letter "L," and went forth to find water.

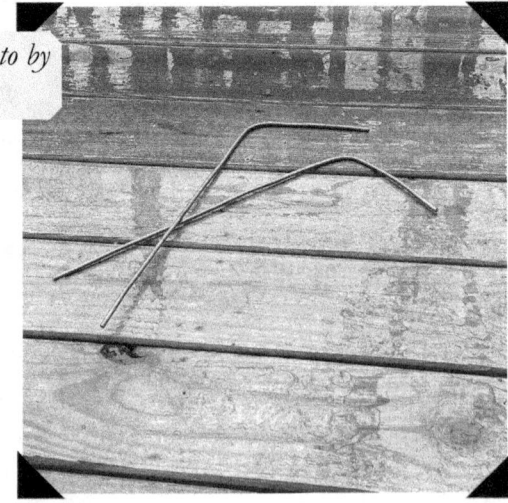

L-Rods (Plum Branch, SC. Photo by Jan Willis)

And I struck out, totally. I had been told by numerous websites that the rods would either cross or open up if I walked slowly over an underground water source. Didn't happen. Even when I walked over the spot where I knew the water line ran from the well to the house, I got nothing. Zip! Thoroughly discouraged, I did what any modern researcher would do. I went back online for more study.

I came across some sites that, at the time, seemed quite wacko. They said you could dowse for the presence of spirits. That was even stranger than dowsing for water. I at least *believed* in water. Spirits? Not so much.

I also found a site that talked about dowsing for Earth energy. Now, that was more up my alley! While skeptical about certain human practices like dowsing, I have always been a confirmed nature mystic. So, armed with my L-rods, confident that Barb was taking a nap and wouldn't see my foolishness, I started off across sections of our woods' paths and the small yard we had cleared from the forest around our home.

One step—nothing. Another step— the rods suddenly crossed all by themselves.

There, right in front of our house, I received the shock of my life. While concentrating as best I knew how, I took the step that has probably changed me forever. One step—nothing. Another step—the rods suddenly crossed, all by themselves, and this in the hands of someone who up until that moment had been highly skeptical.

I stepped back and tried it again. Same thing. I straightened them out in my hands and walked a little farther. A few steps later, they moved again. It was almost as if I was crossing a stream from one shore to the other. When measured, the apparent river of energy turned out to be about 85 inches wide. When I came from one direction and reached the "shore" of the energy, the rods crossed. When I crossed over and came back from the other side, they crossed again.

I asked whatever "Powers That Be" if this was an underground stream—kind of a prayer "To Whom It May Concern." Maybe I had found water. But no, when I stepped onto the area with water on my mind, nothing happened. The only way I could get the rods to move by themselves was to concentrate on Earth energy.

Quietly, and only to myself, I asked "someone," or "something," or "whatever," which direction the energy was flowing. Both rods slowly turned to the southeast. When I asked what direction the energy was coming from, they slowly turned to the northwest.

I walked about 50 or 60 feet "upstream" and tried again. Same thing. Eighty-five inches across. I drew an imaginary line through our house, lined up a tall tree for bearings, went around to the backyard and tried again. There, too. I continued downhill, taking bearings on trees so as to keep a straight line, and kept measuring. Every place, 85 inches. Same results. There was a perfectly straight line of energy that ran through our property from northwest to southeast. I had, in fact, discovered a ley line, or what is now more and more being called an Energy Ley.

Since that time, I have traced the line on a topographical map and dowsed it out as far as at least a mile in both directions. Sometimes it takes a little walking to find it, even with a large-scale map. But when I do—85 inches every time! I have also extended the line cross-country, on a road map, and was amazed to discover the number of Native American sacred sites it bisected.

Thoroughly spooked and out of breath, I waited until Barb joined me to repeat the exercise. I kept saying to her, "Watch my

Plotting a Ley Line — Barb and I, Plum Branch, SC (photo by Jan Willis).

hands. Make sure I'm not moving them!" I even tried to get the rods to stand still. But every time, without exception, even with my eyes closed so I wouldn't know when I came to the edge of a line, when I crossed the flow of that powerful Earth energy, the rods crossed of their own accord. I couldn't make them *not* do it. It was as if they were hitting a wall and collapsing in on themselves.

Once the ice was broken—the skeptic converted, so to speak— the sky became the limit. I could ask for the presence of water and the rods would cross whenever I stood over an underground source. I could even deduce the direction of flow and determine, by a series of bracketing questions, how deep the water was.

I stood over our well, for instance, and figured out how many feet down it was. When I checked the figures left by the driller, I found I had come within five feet. Over and over again, with expanding confidence, I discovered that there was almost no limit to what I could discover about the "magical" outdoors that I had lived in all my life. I delighted in asking a question to which there was no way to discover the answer until I could verify it after the fact. I have rarely been disappointed.

Mysteriously, I also discovered the presence of what others might call "spirits." About a year after I had been dowsing almost daily and had grown a lot more accomplished, I discovered a way to actually communicate with those forces or entities that have been given many names by many cultures. I discovered that they are very real, and both willing and able to communicate with us.

Our language is insufficient. Words such as *meta*physical (outside of human sense perception) and *super*natural (above the natural) have been so misused that in some conversations they are employed to denote condescension and even ridicule. But there are no other words yet in common use that can replace them, so I'm stuck with them.

To make a long story short, my spiritual journey that began with the words, "I will not let you go until you bless me," was fulfilled. My prayer was answered. The best way for me to explain it is to say that I discovered my Holy Grail. I found God. Not the old, limited, Christian definition of "God" that I labored under for my whole life, but an expanded, spiritual, scientific, reality-based, emotional, physical, and psychological presence that was understood by the ancients but lost in the mad rush to embrace left-brained intellectualism that has been with us for the last few hundred years. It was there all along. I just never previously took the time to find it. When I finally did, there it was, hiding in plain sight.

I don't claim that my experience was somehow unique, although, in a very real sense, *every* human experience of the divine is unique. I don't claim to know "the" way to God or spiritual insight. My only claim is that my experience worked for me. It satisfied my personal quest.

I shouldn't have been surprised that my journey led to spiritual insights gleaned from nature. Nature is, in a very real sense, our creator—our entrance into this material realm. Our bodies originated there, and will return, upon our death. But is there more to us than just our bodies?

Yes! We are much more than our bodies, and I think we can find evidence of this as we finally arrange the flowers we gathered along our journey together. When we do so, they reveal quite an unexpected, but revealing, picture.

Cosmo and Me

Chapter 8:
Arranging the Flowers
Gathered Along the Way

That Age is best, which is the first,
When Youth and Blood are warmer;
But being spent, the worse, and worst times,
Still succeed the former.

—*Robert Herrick*

We began this journey together with some advice: "First, gather the flowers. Make sure you get a full array of colors. You can arrange them in a beautiful display later, after you have time to see how they fit together and highlight each other. That's what journeys are for—to gather the flowers of experience."

It's now time to arrange the flowers we've gathered from our memories of the last seven decades. I've shared mine. You undoubtedly have many more.

Probably without realizing it, we've learned something even before we begin the task of organizing our bouquets. By relating, and sometimes agonizing over, the events that shaped the last half century or so, events with which we are all at least somewhat familiar, even if we didn't live through all of them, it soon becomes obvious that some of the most beautiful and fragrant flowers grow way back in the swamp. Some of the most prolific spring up unexpectedly from the manure pile. Tough times don't always make for tough people. But tough people always grow from tough times.

As I look back on my life, and as you look back on yours after recounting the experiences we just shared, it is surprising that some of the lowest points brought forth the most-remembered and most-appreciated lessons. Those lessons are the flowers that grew back in the swamps and out of the manure piles. We may not know why, exactly, but those tough time may be the reason we were born in the first place.

I have a theory that I have often written about before, but I share it again now because it is so important. It's just a theory. I'm not claiming any divine revelation that might spark a new religion. But at the very least, it certainly demands some consideration.

If you've come this far with me, please stay the course. It might feel as though what follows is a sudden turn to religion or philosophy, but it's not. You see, each flower we gathered represents something much bigger than a single memory. It represents *purpose*. There is a *reason* we picked it and stored it safely in our memory banks. It meant something to us. And as we begin to arrange them all, a pattern unfolds. They are pixels, if you will, that form a moving picture on the TV screen of life. Individually, each pixel doesn't seem like much. But together they form a moving picture that has purpose and direction—that tells a story.

So this theory begins with the notion that every individual life has purpose. I'm familiar, of course, with the idea held by many scientists that life is a cosmic accident, but I just don't buy it. A lifetime of experience and counseling more people that I can count has convinced me that there are simply too many coincidences and synchronicities that cannot be explained. I see history as a pattern and individual lifetimes as a wave within that pattern. I cannot make any sense of the notion that there isn't *something* behind it all. Life is too complex to have evolved on its own.

Is that scientific on my part? I used to say no and chalk it up to something called faith. But I just can't do that anymore. I think there *is* evidence. The problem is that it is not the kind of evidence you can slice up and put under a microscope or tease out of mathematical equations.

Werner Heisenberg, one of the premier physicists and, dare I say it, philosophers, of the 20th century, once said, "What we observe is not nature itself, but nature exposed to our method of questioning."

Science is a wonderful process of inquiry and methodology. It is capable of great feats and is the crown jewel of human intellect. But it is not without its shortcomings, and one of them is this: The tools scientists employ to such great effect are designed to observe and measure evidence that exists within the confines of the material universe, and the material universe only. They are totally ineffective when it comes to examining subjects such as love, for instance, or morality, or ethics, or even great art. Science can tell you what musical or artistic methods were employed by great musicians or painters. But it cannot compose a Brahms symphony or a Mona Lisa. The best it can do is imitate or produce an exact copy.

That is precisely why artificial intelligence is so dangerous. It is not capable of the ineffable leap from the material world to the world of inspiration and intuition—from the *physical* to the *meta*physical—from the *natural* to the *super*natural. AI is certainly predictable and dependable when it comes to preserving the status quo. But it cannot jump the fence and land in the field of complete originality and genius.

As we have seen throughout the course of this book, human beings muck about in the metaphorical equivalent of swamps and manure piles for much of their lives. But out of such experiences grew the beautiful flowers of experience, insight, and wisdom.

How can that happen?

It was in searching for an answer to that question that I decided to put my faith in human purpose and meaning. I have come to believe that "mucking about" is precisely why humans exist in the first place. It is what we were born to do. It's our purpose in life— indeed, it is *the* purpose to life, as far as I'm concerned. It appears now, given our current state of knowledge, that we are the first thinking, intelligent, sentient, biological species on Earth to have evolved to the point where we can "muck about" with alacrity and benefit, and it is only "mucking about" that can produce spiritual growth. It might well be the reason we decided to get born in the first place.

"Wait a minute!" you say. "What do you mean we 'decided' to get born! I don't ever remember being given that opportunity."

That leads to the theory I want to propose. I put forth the idea that life has purpose. It follows, then, that we might have had a say in what that purpose is.

Think of it this way.

What if Consciousness pervades the universe? What if Consciousness is the first cause of the universe? What if saying, "In the beginning, God created the Heavens and the earth" is exactly the same as saying, "In the beginning, *Consciousness* created the Heavens and the earth?"

Picture "everything that is" as a rotating circle with something we'll call "Source" as its center. In the Source there is perfect unity, perfect peace. It's the stillpoint of the circle. There is no individuality. All is one, beautiful and at rest. There is no conflict or drama. There is no struggle. There is only perfect love and contentment.

But something is missing. How can there be an *experience* of anything outside of perfection? The Source cannot move outside of itself to answer this question—to create such an experience. There is only one way to do that. Part of the Source must separate from perfect unity in order to experience itself. That's where you and I come in. We left the unity of Source to experience duality in material existence.

Try reading the Bible by substituting a few words here and there to help free us from traditional interpretations that can cloud our minds.

> *In the beginning, Consciousness created the Heavens and the earth*
> ...
> *And Source saw that it was good.*

Stop right there! How could Source see that "it was good?" "Good" is a term that can only exist in the presence of its opposite. There can be no "good" without comparing it to something that is "bad." In other words, read in this way, the Bible says that its original authors, the ancient elders, understood the wisdom of the fact that duality pervades all of materialism. It is the backdrop of all life—the vase that holds the flowers of life's experience. When Adam and Eve, our mythical ancestors, "ate of the fruit of the tree of good and evil," they were experiencing duality. As do we all. All the time. Every minute of every day, we experience individuality.

How did we get here? We moved out from the Source, away from perfect unity. We separated from Source. We separated from "God," using the words of the ancient religious texts. It was a courageous decision—a heroic decision. Thus, we are all heroes. As Jesus said it so clearly, "Know ye not that ye are Gods?"

So, what kind of environment did we find ourselves in once we began to take on material existence? I call it the environment of individual consciousness. Both Albert Einstein and Stephen Hawking called it "The Mind of God."

We had no mass yet, of course, either physical or metaphysical. I sometimes say we were a little "thicker" or "heavier." Perhaps we hadn't yet visualized where we were going or what we would look like. But we were probably aware that we would, eventually.

Understand, now, that this is an extreme simplification of a process we don't have the intelligence or vocabulary to describe. But imagine that it is at least a possibility. What could an environment such as the "Mind of God" possibly be like?

There would still be complete unity, but there would also be an awareness that something we can only call uniqueness and individuality really do exist. What is it like to be different for the first time? What is it like to have an individual thought? What does it feel like to be alone? What is it like to have an individual, unique experience?

These kinds of thoughts are impossible within the parameters of the Source. There's only one way to find out. You have to travel onward.

When you do so, your journey now takes you through the first defining field. It's a place wherein you begin to take on shape. Not mass. Not yet. But you grow a little "heavier" as you begin to transform yourself into something truly unique and separate.

In previous books I took a cue from the ancient Hindu Rishis and called this place of transformation the *Akashic Field*. Everything that we know and experience around us, every rock, tree, and flower, every person, every animal, every bird and fish was first conceived in Akasha.

There is no *real* individuality there, but the *concept* of individuality exists. There is what we can only call "metaphysical" mass. We can understand the *idea* of individuality but have not yet totally achieved it. We might say that we have begun to understand that unique *individuality* leads to unique *experience*. Once we pass through the Akashic Field, we become something different. We now have direction or trajectory. We are aiming for something. We have been launched towards a target.

Past the Akashic Field lies a totally different realm. This is the region scientists call *Quantum Reality*, having discovered it through mathematics only about a hundred years ago. They have only begun to explore it.

Sir James Hopwood Jeans was a brilliant English physicist, astronomer, and mathematician. He once said: "Humanity is at the very beginning of its existence—a new-born babe, with all the unexplored potentialities of babyhood; and until the last few moments its interest has been centered absolutely and exclusively on its cradle and feeding bottle."

I have quoted Jeans many times before. This is one of my favorites: "The universe begins to look more like a great *thought* than a great *machine*." That's why I like to call Quantum Reality the place of "Thoughts and Intentions."

Quantum Reality is a place of potential. Humans don't really live there, but *from* there the potential for any one human can be

realized. That potential will be manifested when "a human," you, "collapses" into the material environment we now experience. To do that it must pass through the newly discovered Higgs Field.

Physicists are excited about the Higgs Field. It's a brand-new discovery that was made possible through the CERN super collider. As yet there is no universal, accepted definition of the field, but it's there.

In simplistic terms, when energy passes through the Higgs Field, it emerges on our side with mass. Mass and energy are the same thing in different forms. Expressed mathematically it looks like this: $E=mc^2$. (Energy equals, or is the same as, mass times the speed of light squared.)

Welcome to life in our perception realm—the world of the five senses. Now scientists can start measuring things.

But even this world has its hidden realms. Besides what we *can* see, there are possibilities of things we *can't* see, such as the Multiverse, in its infinite capacity for creativity. Given the limitlessness of infinity, and the limits of finite mass, there exist all possible manifestations of every single possibility—all kinds of permutations mass can take. Perhaps even an infinite number of "yous" are living their own lives, gathering their own flowers, all in woeful ignorance that doppelgangers in parallel universes are writing books like this with vastly different endings. We just don't know.

If any of this is even close to the Truth, it leaves us with some penetrating questions. To attempt to answer some of these, let's return to quoting the Bible, but changing a word here and there in order to break away from the habit of traditional interpretations.

By the way, I use the Bible only because it is home to me. I could easily derive the same conclusions from the wisdom literature of any number of traditional religions. If you have trouble with this, please try to separate the wisdom of ancient elders from the religions that have grown up around the texts. It's not the elder's fault that their insights have been corrupted. Try to hear them with fresh minds and hearts.

That being said, this first insight might come as a bit of a shock.

People have often asked me whether or not I believe in Heaven and Hell. They are usually either relieved or shocked when I say, "Yes." Religious folks are relieved that I'm not a heretic. Non-believers think I'm naïve. But my definition of Heaven and Hell is quite different from theirs.

Take the concept of Hell, for instance. Is it a place of eternal torment and torture for those who don't shape up during their lifetimes? Of course not! How could a "good" God even conceive of such a horrible idea?

So what, then, is Hell?

What those who believe in Hell agree on is that it's a place of separation from God.

But is that not a pretty good definition of life on Earth? Don't humans on this material plain and planet feel separated from God? Isn't that why religions go to such lengths to try to bring God and humans together? Isn't the idea of union with God the very essence of religious dogma and doctrine?

Think about it. If Hell is separation from the unity of Source and peace, and we live in a material word that majors in individuality and chaos, where do we live? In Hell! There is no other way to say it.

Even the Bible agrees. Consider 1st John 5:19: "We know that we are of God, and that the whole world is under the power of the evil one." You can't get much more straightforward than that. (We'll get to the identity of "the evil one" in a minute.)

If we have the courage to break away from tradition and think in these terms, it answers a lot of questions.

First of all, God doesn't *send* anyone to Hell as punishment. We *choose* to come here in order to fulfill a higher purpose—that of experiencing individuality. It's a noble cause to enter into separation from "God" in order to benefit the Source. Wasn't that exactly the mission Christians say engaged Jesus? Didn't he willingly leave the glories of Heaven, of Source, to separate himself in order to be born as a man?

> *Have this mind among yourselves, which is yours in Christ Jesus, who, though he was in the form of God, did not count equality with God a thing to be grasped, but emptied himself, by taking the form of a servant, being born in the likeness of men. And being found in human form, he humbled himself by becoming obedient to the point of death, even death on a cross.*
>
> —Philippians 2:5

And then, having accomplished all this, was he not supposed to have said that *his* mission was also *our* mission? "Pick up your cross daily and follow me."

A moment ago, we said we would soon take up the identity of what the Bible calls "the evil one," the one who controls this material perception realm. Religions call this entity the devil, Satan, which means "the deceiver," Iblis, Mara, or a host of other names. Who is he?

Hang on here, because the answer is not what you think.

If the complete peace of unity is found *in* the source, then it stands to reason that it's opposite, the chaos of disunity, is found *outside* the Source. And what is the basis of chaos and disunity? Human ego, the inevitable curse of individuality, even as it is also obligatory if we are to achieve our goal of individual experience in this field of duality.

Could it be that at the root of all evil is human ego, which has deceived us into thinking we are individual beings—that we are alone—that we are separated from the Source? It may be a *necessary* deception because without it we could never have experienced true individuality and gone about the task of gathering flowers on our lonely journey through life. But it is a deception just the same.

We are here on Earth to learn the lessons of duality, the "knowledge of good and evil." But we are caught in what feels like a divine battle of competing spiritual forces. We still need to "earn our daily bread by the sweat of our brow." It's just that we have turned our curse into a search for meaning. We want to get back to Paradise.

In short, according to this theory, we are all "demon possessed." But the "demon" who "possesses" us is one of our own making. It is human ego. Ego inspires us to do what we do and behave the way we behave. But ego, again using a biblical phrase from Revelation 12:2, "knows that his time is short." Ego only lasts a lifetime. When we die and return to the unity of Source, there is no longer any room for ego.

So our lives here on Earth are caught between two opposing forces—the *experience* of ego and the *memory* of unity. In a world of dualities, how could it be otherwise?

The universe is bigger than we realize. As a matter of fact, the universe is simply one cell in the immense body of the Multiverse, which is a material manifestation of the Source. Here on Earth the battle between good and evil, the inevitable battle of duality, is raging. Earth may be the *domain* of the so-called "curse" of separation and chaos, but that domain itself has been called, by God, or Consciousness itself, "good." The ancients recognized it, calling it "Mother Earth," the creation of the goddess of wisdom. It contains the Divine Spark that the devil, human ego, strives to overcome and conquer.

A verse that sums up the whole situation, and, indeed, describes the whole theory I have just put forth, might be this one: "Light has come into the world, but men loved darkness rather than light, because their deeds were evil" (John 3:19).

Is it any wonder that our nighttime dreams are so full of worries and fears?

But the old texts considered that as well. Again, quoting the wisdom of the elders who wrote the Bible, this time from 1st John 4:18: "Perfect love casts out fear."

This rather novel reinterpretation of the familiar Christian approach to the notion of *theodicy*, or why bad things happen to good people, doesn't depend on two supernatural entities, God and the devil, duking it out on Earth for supremacy. It doesn't try to explain a scenario wherein people are punished for their supposed sin and rewarded for virtue. It simply uses traditional terms—"God," "devil," "Heaven," and "Hell"—to describe how the mysterious and ineffable *Source of All That Is* might, through eternal Consciousness, grow by exploring the perception of material duality, something that isn't possible in a "place" where the peace of perfect unity is all that there is.

When I call this life "Hell," I don't mean it is always terrible or some kind of divine punishment. That might be the way *you* have been trained to think about it since childhood. But it's not what *I* mean.

By the same token, I don't think of "Heaven" as a place of eternal reward. I think of it as the "place" of the Source, perfect unity, from which we came, and to which we return after a short sojourn here on this material plain.

"God" isn't a divine being "out there" somewhere, who "knows when you've been bad or good, so be good for goodness' sake." According to this interpretation, "God" is Source, seeking to grow by experiencing a life that is not possible without leaving the womb of eternal peace and taking individuality upon itself.

The "devil" is ego, the inescapable result of individuality. Only an individual entity--in other words, us--can think of itself as separate and apart. Individuals may feel alone and lonely, they may experience fear and dread, they might let ego run wild from time to time, but even that is something that cannot be experienced in any other way except through, in the words of the Bible, "being born in fashion as an [individual human being]" with all the rights and privileges, and fears and hurts, that entails.

What we have been exploring throughout this whole book is a possible answer to life's greatest question: *Why are we here?*

Simply put, we are here to "muck about." We are here to slug through the swamps of individuality and dig around in the manure pile of human shortcomings. While "mucking about" in those environments, we occasionally find some beautiful flowers of experience, and in arranging those flowers we discover we have some-how managed to build a beautiful bouquet of wisdom that could not have been possible to create in any other way.

People who have undergone a near death experience often re-late similar stories. They see a bright light. They are greeted by some kind of spiritual guide. They feel an inexpressible love and peace that is so powerful they usually don't want to leave. But they also relate that they experience a life review. Their whole life flash-es before their eyes. Meaning is thus laid bare.

I have heard this story from dozens of people and read about it in hundreds of memoirs. I have come to believe that this "life review" is real. It represents the flowers of experience, the flowers of wisdom, that we have gathered during our life journey. During our "life review" we present those experiences to the Source. And upon receiving them, the Source grows a little by learning some-thing it could not have learned without our help. That, indeed, might just be the whole reason we are born, we live, and we die. We have come to "muck about" while we gather the experiences of individuality that produce wisdom.

And perhaps, just perhaps, when it is all over, we really *will* hear something akin to the traditional words of the Christian burial ser-vice. Maybe we *will* receive that welcome plaudit, "Well done, good and faithful servant. Enter into the joy of eternal life!"

But maybe the words will be changed to, "*Re*-enter the joy of eternal life!"

And maybe there will be one more phrase added as well: "Thanks for the Flowers!"

"Thanks for the Flowers!" (Photo by Jan Willis)

www.ingramcontent.com/pod-product-compliance
Lightning Source LLC
Chambersburg PA
CBHW060511130626
46553CB00002B/459